A ROMAN LIFE

RUTILIUS

GALLICUS

On Paper

&

In Stone

EXETER STUDIES IN HISTORY

General Editors:
Jonathan Barry, Tim Rees *and* T.P. Wiseman

Other paperbacks in this series include:

Roman Political Life, 90 BC–AD 69
edited by T.P. Wiseman (1985)

The Administration of the Roman Empire, 241 BC–AD 193
edited by David Braund (1988)

Satire and Society in Ancient Rome
edited by Susan H. Braund (1989)

Flavius Josephus: *Death of an Emperor*
translated with an Introduction and Commentary
by T.P. Wiseman (1991)

Historiography and Imagination: Eight Essays on Roman Culture
T.P. Wiseman (1994)

Roman Public Buildings
edited by Ian M. Barton (new edition 1995)

Roman Domestic Buildings
edited by Ian M. Barton (1996)

Phlegon of Tralles' Book of Marvels
translated with an Introduction and Commentary
by William Hansen (1996)

Figuring Out Roman Nobility
by John Henderson (1997)

Roman Drama and Roman History
by T.P. Wiseman (1998)

The front cover illustration shows Marius in his old age: *from a nineteenth-century cartoon, with details from Figures 1 and 6 (see page ix).*

A ROMAN LIFE

RUTILIUS GALLICUS
On Paper
&
In Stone

JOHN HENDERSON

UNIVERSITY
of
EXETER
PRESS

First published in 1998 by
University of Exeter Press
Reed Hall, Streatham Drive
Exeter, Devon EX4 4QR
UK

British Library Cataloguing in Publication Data
A catalogue record for this book
is available from the British Library

ISBN 0 85989 565 3

Typeset in Monotype Sabon by
Exe Valley Dataset, Exeter

Printed and bound in Great Britain by
Short Run Press Ltd, Exeter

uxori et filiis:
diu multumque dubitaui

(4KLM)

CONTENTS

CONTENTS

ILLUSTRATIONS

Cover and prelims. J. Leech, 'Marius in his old age', in C.A. à Beckett (*c.* 1860) *A Comic History of Rome,* London: 266.

Figure 1a and b (pp. 4–5). The Rutilius Gallicus inscription from Ephesus (*ILS* 9499=*IE* III. 114, no. 715). (a) Marble block from the base of a statue: 0.75 m high, 575 mm wide, 0.55 m thick; crisp lettering in Roman capitals 2^{1}/$_{2}$–5 cm high; found built into Byzantine city wall near the theatre=Keil (1914) 195 Figure 23. (b) Line-drawing.

Figure 2a–d (pp. 12–13). The Rutilius inscription *in situ* at Ephesus. Photographs courtesy of Dr Hans Taeuber.

Figure 3 (p. 21). *Sestertius* with bust of Domitian and saecular games of 88=*BMCRE* 2. 425, Plate 78. 7, cf. p. 393: (obv.) bust of Domitian: *IMP-[ERATOR] CAES[AR] DOMIT[IANVS] AUG[VSTVS] GERM[ANICVS] P[ONTIFEX] M[AXIMVS] TR[IBVNICIA] P[OTESTATE] VIII CENS[OR] PER[PETVVS] [PATER PATRIAE]* ('The Emperor Caesar Domitian Augustus Germanicus, Chief Priest, holding the power of a tribune for the eighth time, Censor without term [, Father of the Father-land]'); (rev.) Domitan bare-headed and wearing toga stands to right, sacrificing from a *patera* over a lighted and garlanded altar; on right, *uictimarius* holds pig; on left, topless *Tellus* reclines to the right, holding cornucopias in right hand and stretching out her left; in background, lyre-player advances to right and flute-player advances to left: *CO[N]S[ULE] XIIII LVD[OS] SAEC[VLARES] FEC[IT]* ('In his thirteenth consulship he held the saecular games').

Figure 4 (p. 23). 'Palatine Gate', Turin=Model in the Museo della Civiltà Romana, Rome, *INR* 73. 944, cf. Zanker (1988) 329, Figure 257.

Figure 5a, b and c (pp. 26, 28, 30–31). Maps of the city of Rome; Italy; the Roman Empire. The maps locate what is mentioned in the book.

Figure 6 (p. 71). MS. Madrid, Biblioteca Nacional 3678 (written 1417/8), folio 71 *verso* with part of Statius, *Siluae* 1. 4. 61–98, cf. Dunston (1967) Plate IX (a).

Figure 7 (p. 91). Asklepios, after the cult-statue at Epidaurus, by Thrasymedes of Paros, on trihemidrachma of Epidaurus, *c.* 350–00 BCE=*LIMC* II. 1, *Asklepios* 84 (Moulage Winterthur Stadtbibliothek Phot. *LIMC*): (*obv.*) Apollo; (*rev.*) topless Asklepios enthroned in left profile, right arm outstretched above a snake, left arm raised holding a vertical staff; a dog lies against the chair.

Figure 8 (p. 136). Aeneas leans on his spear while Iapyx tends his leg-wound, Venus in the background; Vespasianic wall-painting from Pompeii, Casa di Sirico = Museo Nazionale di Napoli *inv.* 9009, cf. *LIMC* I. 1, *Aineias* 174.

PREFACE

Rutilius Gallicus is, I think, unique as a figure from the heyday of the Roman Empire who *can* be studied in detail through both text and inscription and who *isn't* part of an emperor's family.[1] As well as taking us on a tour across the city of Rome and the provinces, and through Flavian history and culture, Gallicus appears by turns as a formal public servant, a delicate amateur poet-rhetorician, a workaholic chasing an early grave, the darling of his people, the strong-man of the tyrant Domitian, the miraculously resurrected patient of Apollo, and a soldier-hero of the Empire. How long could it last?

On the one hand, we can read the stone on which a hopeful junior colleague had Gallicus' career with the legions written up into a personalized history of the first century CE, imagine what *a* Gallicus took normality to be, and guess his expectations. On the other, we can see him through a poet's eyes, squeezed for symbolic value as trope for the Roman universe, seized to try and make sense of Rome. Between these competing versions of Gallicus, we can ponder *A Roman Life*.

That's what this book is about. But I know that people like authors to say a bit more these days about what *they* are about. So here is a potted history, or (better) 'archaeology'. Obviously, I hope you'll recover from it— and stick around. The book grew from a paper given at a cracking Cambridge Graduate Literary Seminar series on *Siluae* I. It kept dying and sputtering back into a half-life of misgivings, as *my* life sagged beneath the burden of being (Assistant) Tutor in my College, until it struck me that juxtaposing poetic and epigraphic texts could bring *pharmacological* reading to *A Roman Life*. Timely acclamation of Professor J. Derrida as honorary 'Doctor' of my University became tonic and aspic for this *writing as poison and cure*. In Pindar, the gods foster the mythic hero with the *balm of honey*, called '*blameless poison*' (*Olympians* 6. 46f., 'Iamos' with *ios*, cf. Stern (1970) 334); to turn *his* hero into myth, Statius has the god of medicine apply 'every *kindly poison*' (vv. 103f.), and that is just what Statius' writing does for Gallicus, too.[2] Through Gallicus, as Statius himself will alert us, mythopoeic writing heals and holes the Roman world, by opening subjectivity to metonymic metaphor and then taking the con-sequences. This individual gives onto the expanse of culture along a broad spectrum of frequencies. By contrast, the career inscription for Gallicus registers him as one ant functioning in an imperial myriad. His existence is stamped into the world-dealing of the hierarchized power-system, peremptorily plugged into the dykes and drills of an army of occupation's crisis and tedium. This subjectivity is run along the rails of rank, in the clipped poetics of *officialese*. If this heretical book is about reinstating lyrical reading into the reception of Roman political rhetoric, it is also about the restitution of religious discourse to the heart of Roman poetry, and as such about life and times within Roman temporality. So where am I coming from and did I make it in one piece?

> Hudson left Paris convinced he was cured of AIDS.
> Back in the United States, Hudson, a life-long Republican, attended a state dinner at the White House. Noting that the actor had lost weight, an old friend from Hollywood expressed concern about his health.
> 'I caught some flu bug when I was filming in Israel,' Hudson assured his friend, Nancy Reagan. 'I'm feeling fine now.'[3]

How individuals associated with social power and prestige handle intimations of (their, so our) mortality feeds back into our construction of social power, and our consequent ascription of prestige to particuar individuals. For as everyone in the playground knows, the stone that the paper enfolds *blunts the scissors*.

I hope that hits the spot. I owe Mary Beard for help with epigraphy, K. M. Coleman for her meticulous corrections of a draft, Peter Wiseman who read and commented on the manuscript as scrupulously and inventively as ever, and a fair number of friends for comments they won't remember giving. Simon Baker, Genevieve Davey, Richard Willis, Anna Henderson and the rest of the team at *UEP* have been great to work with again.

A Roman Life *can be read either in the running order, or by starting from chapter five, where Statius' poem gets the works, and then going back to the inscription and the various histories that occupy the first four chapters. I'd dearly like to know which way round works better and why, but I guess there are plenty of other options. For example, chapter twenty swiftly introduces* Book I, *while chapter nineteen introduces the introduction to* Book I; *and the* Appendix *introduces Pindar's thanksgiving poetry, which obviously came first, by more than half a millennium.*

All dates are CE unless otherwise indicated. References to lines of Statius Siluae 1. 4 *appear in the form 'v. 1', 'vv. 1–131'.*

Introduction

The emperor Domitian's *Prefect of Rome*, C. Rutilius Gallicus, once recovered from grave illness, some form of catatonic, life-threatening breakdown. This became the moment for a celebratory lyric poem from Statius: *Siluae* 1. 4. Statius' work is attracting enthusiastic revaluation, not just for his epic poetry. His occasional poems, the *Siluae*, are also being read with new interest as today's cultural historians look for 'insider' perspectives on the fabric of Roman social life. Gallicus' psychic trauma marks him out, as it does any of us, as a *person*. (Remember, you're amazing.) I don't know that he would like us or be liked, but he's a Roman with plenty of life left in him.

For a start, both Gallicus and 'his' poem turn up in all sorts of scholarly discussions of Roman history and Latin literature. Here are some examples: in *Sittengeschichte* (the history of manners), the *Siluae* have always been crucial texts in the study of politesse, taste, ideology in imperial court circles. The poem is itself important as a classic *soteria*, or 'thanksgiving for recovery', and gets studied to see how tightly or loosely it coheres with other examples. In literary history, Rutilius Gallicus' is a suggestive profile for authorship in the cosmopolis of Rome, even if his writings (poetry and oratory) are all lost without trace. For political historians, the shape of Gallicus' career bears on the development of the imperial *consilium* (kitchen cabinet) and *praefectura urbis* (police department), on the system of imperial priesthood, and on the divinity of the emperor. For historians of ancient religion, Gallicus' poem sheds light on the saecular games of 88, and on the launch of the cult of Asklepios into efflorescence in the early second century. Above

1

all, perhaps, 'for fanciers of senatorial careers', Gallicus has proved a favourite prosopographical challenge, and here our chief Rutilius Gallicus inscription has come into its own (*ILS* 9499).[4]

These topics will all get the treatment. Gallicus' poem twines together the cultural charisma of the literary scene and its aesthetic design for life, with those of government business and administrative power at Rome, and triggers Roman reflection upon Roman cultural history and aspirations. In the form of a particular 'nosopolitics', Statius presents general terms for thinking the theurgy of the emperor, whose godhead radiates salvation through his world, or else fails to function and undoes his sway.[5] Divine medication of the loyal prefect can stand in for Domitian's transcendental mediation in the vicissitudes of all his subjects' Roman lives. The planet depends on his vindication. Let Statius' music strain every chord to live up to its billing as the healing force of the universe, whatever the risk of capsize into bathos. For now, let's just note that Gallicus' poem will re-cycle Virgilian and Horatian scenarios, and turn to Pindaric and Ovidian precedents, to make a culture-myth with, and of, him (chapters 5–20, and *Appendix*). But first we turn to the inscription, and follow Gallicus' career through the last years of the Julio-Claudians, then through the conflagrations of the civil wars that raised Domitian's father Vespasian to rule the world (chapters 1–4).

1

The Words in the Stone

For whatever reason, Gallicus—born in the late 20s, dead in 92—
escapes stigmatization of Domitian's agents and hatchet-men in later
recriminations from Tacitus, Pliny and Juvenal.[6] Outside Statius, *Siluae*
1. 4, he is known to texts only at Juv. 13. 157, where he is caricatured
only as 'Routi*n*ius Gallicus—always living off other people's misery—in
court'. This may show he had been no villain. But maybe he just died in
good time, well before Domitian's assassination and Statius' decease in
96. Or else he was small fry, all along . . . Between Juvenal, Statius, and
several inscriptions, Gallicus has, at any rate, registered as an 'item' in
Roman history and Latin literature: he is '*PIR*³ 3. 148f., R. 167', '*RE*
1A. 1255 *Rutilius* 19', '*PME* 1. 450 I. 48', and '*IE* III. 715' (See
Bibliography *ad init.*).

For the great Roman historian Sir Ronald Syme, the Gallicus
inscription put up at Ephesus by an equestrian officer in *c.* 70/1 yields
an 'epigraphical harvest'.[7] 'Gallicus was previously thought to have
been adlected by Vespasian on the grounds that the sketch of his career
given by Statius . . . suggests that he was originally in the equestrian
service, and does not allude to any senatorial office held by him before
the praetorship. But the inscription found at Ephesus . . . shows clearly
that he went through the whole of the senatorial cursus.'[8] Modern
French philology actually began with the *Révue de Philologie* heading
its very first volume with Desjardins' proclamation of the 'Nécessité' for
epigraphy to rescue the literary text; he topped this by composing a
completed *cursus honorum* (an epitaph) for Gallicus![9] Now we have
ILS 9499 (Figures 1a and b), you might think we can get on to the

3

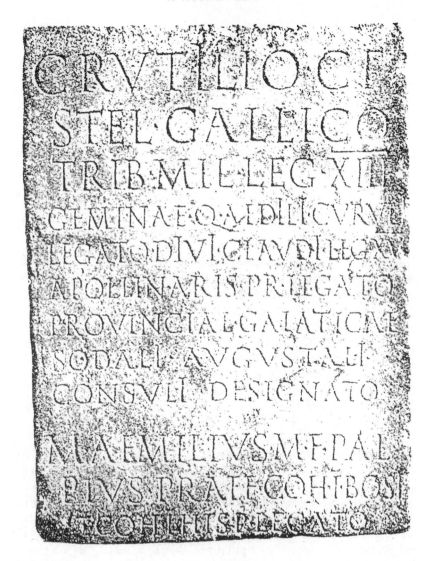

Figure 1a. The Rutilius Gallicus inscription from Ephesus (=*ILS* 9499=*IE* III. 114, no. 715).

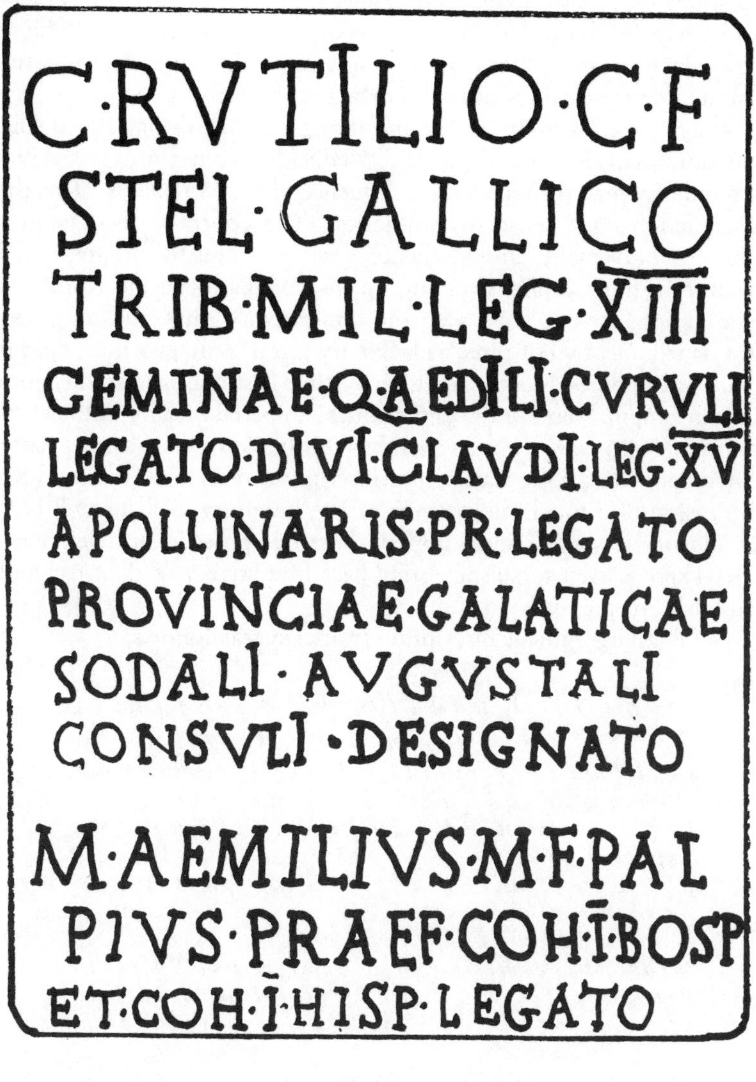

Figure 1b. Line-drawing of the Rutilius Gallicus inscription.

questions that matter: what did Gallicus' profile amount to in practice? And what did Statius' representation of the nexus between profile and experience mean to convey? But answers will depend crucially on disputed interpretations of both poem and inscription, at vital points.

Where once historians spoke and thought of 'the distinguished soldier and statesman, Rutilius Gallicus',[10] Gallicus becomes progressively less of a military man through Syme's sequence of *Roman papers*. 'This thesis is argued from a sense of conviction. The contrary persuasion has obtained universally among classical scholars and historians . . . The Senator Rutilius Gallicus, taking up his command on the Rhine when aged about fifty-two, had seen the armies twice only, and long ago; a year as tribune, two or three as legionary legate'.[11] In general, I hold that Syme was right, or became right, about this. Distinguished soldiers of the Roman Empire were, in the nature of the imperial system, nothing other than statesmen-*cum*-civil servants. But this book argues—from a sense of conviction—that both Statius and inscription seek to leave us with the impression of a tough old warhorse. The honorary Gallicus will be like the illusory towers of some imperial fortress, posed as if defending the gate. There is even some suggestion here that literary reading techniques can bush up epigraphy no end.

The Rutilius Gallicus inscription transcribes as follows:

C[aio] · Rutilio · C[ai] · f[ilio]
Stel[latina] · Gallico
trib[uno] · mil[itum] · leg[ionis] · XIII
Geminae · q[uaestori] · aedili · curuli
legato · diui · Claudi · leg[ionis] · XV
Apollinaris · pr[aetori] · legato
prouinciae · Galaticae
sodali · Augustali
consuli · designato
M[arcus] · Aemilius · M[arci] · f[ilius] · Pal[atina]
Pius · praef[ectus] · coh[ortis] · I · Bosp[oranae]
et · coh[ortis] · I · Hisp[aniensis] · legato

To Gaius Rutilius Gallicus, son of Gaius,
of the Stellatine tribe;
military tribune of Legion XIII,
'Two in One'; quaestor; curule aedile;
legate of the divinised Claudius to Legion XV,
'Apollo's Own'; praetor; legate

to the province of Galatia;
member of the priesthood of Augustus;
consul (forthcoming),
Marcus Aemilius Pius, son of Marcus, of the Palatine tribe;
Prefect of Cohort 1, 'Black Seamen',
and of Cohort 1, 'Spanish', to the legate.

To this information about Gallicus' career let us add right away (from other inscriptions) the distended form of his name: Q. Iulius Cordinus *Rutilius Gallicus*. This polyonomastic must have arisen from testamentary adoption, or perhaps bequest, most likely by the Lusitanian Q. *Iulius* Cordus, governor of Aquitania in 68/9; it was used in inscriptions from 74 and 78, but the old *Rutilius Gallicus* turns up after these dates, so it may have been dropped, optional, or just patchy and precarious.[12] Let us notice the proposal that Gallicus' overshadowed father's name was: C. *Rutilius* Secundus, a procurator in Mauretania.[13] And let us add (following Syme (1988) 515, with (1991) 623–9) that Gallicus would in time (have) become: *Pontifex*; *imperial legate in Africa*; *legate of Lower Germany*; and, under Domitian, *proconsul of Asia*; *suffect consul II*; and *Prefect of the City*.

Taken more slowly, this lightning list of shorthand formulae, specially compacted for public display in expensively immortal stone, parades a fair impression of Gallicus' fight, or glide, to the top of the administration. This is, funnily enough, exactly what it was incised and mounted for—part of the publicity which persuaded officer-officials to join in the epigraphic addiction that wrote Rome all over the Empire, sustaining the credibility of the entire apparatus of control with their investment in the system of collaboration through competition. Let's inspect the troops more closely.

'Military tribune of Legion XIII, *Two in One*', the roll-call begins. So Gallicus' first base was at Poetovio between Pannonia and Noricum, the Augustan front-line of defence at the River Drave, superintending the Alpine tribe of Celts, the Taurisci, in their gold-mine of plaguey Noricum. *Legio* XIII, an outfit of Octavian's youth, had marched there under its lion emblem from Upper Germany (where it was stationed in 23) *c.* 45/46, i.e. around the time of Gallicus' military tribunate. There it (and its military tribune, Suetonius' father, Laetus) stayed put, until summoned by Otho to help lose the battle of Bedriacum in 69; sent by Vitellius to build an amphitheatre at Cremona, bedraggled *No. Thirteen* returned to base in time for the procurator of Dalmatia, Cornelius Fuscus, and the Flavian legionary legate in Pannonia, Antonius Primus, to steer it to join Vespasian's cause. On this was built the plan of campaign drawn up at a conference at the Legion's HQ Poetouio. The 13th would hold the centre of the line in the battle 'Before Cremona' and take swift revenge for its previous humiliation there by cremating the city; before returning to base, it would join the suppression of the Gallic revolt of Ciuilis. Later on, *XIII* would march in the Dacian operations of 86–9, i.e. around the probable time of *Silu.* 1. 4. Moving on to Vindobona, soon after 90 (?), the 13th was eventually to base, for good, at Apulum as the garrison of Dacia.[14]

Entwined with the ladder of junior offices at Rome—Gallicus quaestor (in 50/1), and curule aedile (in 52/3)—this soldier's life continues as legionary 'legate of the divinised Claudius to Legion *XV, Apollo's Own*'. This outfit blazons Octavianic tribute to his patron-god; stationed in Pannonia in 23. Gallicus joined the *Fighting Fifteenth* for *c.* 53–4 at its base (from 50) of Carnuntum, commanding under Claudius the front-line of the River Danube and terminus of the road north. In 58, *Apollinaris* went east, for a rôle on Corbulo's sizzling tour of duty in Cappadocia, and, perhaps, through Armenia and into Parthia, even to raid and raze the capital Artaxata, whose walls are washed by the River Araxes . . . Diverted to Alexandria in 66, the governor of Judaea, Vespasian, had them conveyed from there by their legate, his son Titus, to join the Jewish War and invade Galilee: 'the 15th, the old-buddy boys of Vespasian'.[15] *XV* was one of the first two legions to acclaim in his presence Vespasian as emperor, dateline 3 July 69, Judaea.[16] In 71 Titus took the legion back to join *XIII* as garrison of Pannonia, at Carnuntum, where it re-built the camp *c.* 73, and stayed, for use in every Dacian War, including the operations in 86–9, before returning to Parthia with Gallicus' coeval Trajan, and settling forever under Hadrian at the new base of Satala, back in Armenia.[17]

Gallicus was *praetor c.* 55, one of Nero's first batch of appointees; then 'legate to the province of Galatia'. In charge of Galatia (and, if Statius could be believed, of Pamphylia),[18] supporting the command of the swashbuckling generalissimo Domitius Corbulo from Cappadocia, *c.* 56/57/58–62/63/64. *Perhaps* for six of the 'nine years' of fighting that Statius will lump together, and the other three in Pannonia? Thus Gallicus resumed, more or less distantly, or perhaps very closely, his connection with *XV Apollinaris*. Gallicus may have seen no flak, let alone adventured across the Taurus Mountains into Syria or Armenia; equally, he may have fought his way right across the east, as Statius would have it. Maybe Gallicus had a hand in an expansion to the north of the jurisdiction of the governor of Galatia, into Pontus Polemoniacus (in 64); Vespasian's settlement *c.* 74 seems to have further expanded the range eastwards to include Cappadocia and lesser Armenia, but to the south transferred Pisidia to the new province of Lycia-and-Pamphylia.[19] Perhaps Gallicus' spell in Galatia featured some kind of intervention to the south, if nowhere so far as Pamphylia.[20]

'Member of the priesthood of Augustus' from 68, Gallicus took the place suddenly vacated that June by Nero, marked out by emperor Galba as a rising star before the Flavians counted for that much. Tenure was for life, and we know Gallicus died in 91/2 as a *sodalis Augustalis*.[21] We shall come back to Gallicus' position at the time his statue in Ephesus was set up, and *his* experience of 69, 'The Year of the Four Emperors'. For the moment, let us just notice that the 'imminent consulate' [of 71 or 72] featured by the inscription shows off Gallicus as one of the very first officials of Vespasian's new Flavian order, Rome's second dynasty of emperors, whether an appointee of Nero's or Galba's, an alteration or new designation by Vitellius, or whether ratified, reinstated, or selected by Domitian and—that prime Flavian 'deuteragonist' and king-maker—Mucianus, as Vespasian's broker(s), on 1 January 70, or chosen by Vespasian after his arrival in Rome in Fall 70.[22]

If Gallicus was billeted in Ephesus between his arrival after Nero's demise (late 68) and his designation as consul (69? 70? at a pinch, 71?), he will have helped ship the body of the 'false Nero' pretender back to Rome, after *that* stir; and will have seen (or just missed) the despatch of the proconsular governor Fonteius Agrippa (68/9) to turn back the threatened mass barbarian break-in across the Danube, in Moesia. Otherwise, the Flavian procession west to power, first Mucianus from Syria, then Vespasian from Egypt, did not come near Ephesus. Gallicus and Asia just shared in the unnerving waves and counterflows of appointees of one emperor after another, criss-crossing throughout the imperial network in unhinged profusion. Both of 'Gallicus'' legions backed the Flavians. So, presumably, did he—whether helping to run the province, or back in Italy all along (see below).[23]

Gallicus' whizz round the Roman world and up the ladder toward glory would see him a *pontifex* (priest) by the early years of Vespasian's reign.[24] For the census of 73/4, he was sent out as imperial *legatus censibus accipiendis* for Africa.[25] Next, by contrast, as 'legate of Lower Germany' in 76–8 Gallicus may have seen, and directed, military action, against the Bructeri. In 82–4, he took the plum job of the entire imperial

9

administration as proconsul of Asia, one of Domitian's first appointments, and successor to Trajan and Caecina Paetus (in 79/80 and 80/1).[26] In 85, the year when Domitian assumed the censorship, becoming *ces. perpetuus*,[27] he was given a confirmatory second consulate, even if it was only as 'suffect', and so less of an accolade than if his term of office had begun and so dubbed the year. And, under Domitian, probably *c*. 87–91/2, he became Juvenal's *custos Gallicus urbis*, 'Prefect of the City'.[28]

This pinnacle of a Roman functionary's life deserves separate treatment in its own right. First, while Gallicus' inscription is still before us, we will read it as checklist, prompt and matrix for Statius' improvisation of a poetic life for the Prefect. Obviously, that was not the purpose of the inscription *as such*. Rather, the minor lackey Aemilius Pius had played to a Greek gallery for Gallicus, and (by association) for himself. The honorary inscription for Pius' superior had its recognized niche in the Roman order. Whereas late Republican honorific inscriptions 'in which the entire career of offices is set forth' had been 'almost exclusively . . . funerary inscriptions', i.e. *elogia*, in the first century, 'the *cursus honorum*, spelled out and listed in all its individual stages, became a significant means of describing to the public the rank and significance of a living person as well'. Such inscriptions even became 'the typical form in which senators displayed themselves before the public in the imperial period'.[29]

Thus the would-be permanent display of Latin lettering in Ephesus promised that the Romans were here to stay, in this administrative nerve-centre of their province of Asia. We could say Gallicus was actually sent out to fetch round so many frontiers and fronts in order to underwrite the precision of Roman hegemony: 'The Roman Empire was bound together by writing . . . The whole experience of living in the Roman empire, of being ruled by Romans, was overdetermined by the existence of texts.'[30] Rulers and ruled: the rulers were ruled, too, regulated their lives long, in clamorous pyramids of prescription and proscription. Don't get too sorry for him, but a Rutilius Gallicus really was inscribed into the squares he occupied on the board of Roman power; his inscription programmes his priorities, sequences his options, ordains his next moves. Careers are like that, constantly adjusting potential to track-record to challenge to performance. And at least in the public gaze, any success-story, from the Flavian Caesars themselves on down, must perform on cue. To sloganize, we can sum up that Roman epigraphic culture imposed on one and all, as a mandatory term and condition of subjectivity, a customized *discourse of power*. Writing in public distributed roles, conditioned aspirations, and made waves.[31]

Aemilius Pius actually took responsibility for much more than his honorific inscription.[32] For the block of marble on which it is carved, found built into the Byzantine walls of Ephesus by Josef Keil, the long-term Austrian site-manager, 'not far' from the famous vertiginous theatre, was originally the dedicatory face of a statue-base (Figure 2).[33] Bound for glory as one of Vespasian's earliest consuls, Gallicus would leave the province of Asia with a permanent memento. In time, it would prove an earnest of his return to the east (as Domitian's first governor proconsul of Asia in 82–4: vv. 80–3).

What became of the statue we don't know (always assuming there *was* one): if it lived up to the lettering below, it was a first-class turn-out. Punctuation separates each word or short-hand formula; suprascript 'bars' *over*-line, and so designate, the letters that serve for Roman numerals; and thorough, accurate, and decided '*I-longas*' mark instances of the long vowel (e.g. *RUTĪLIUS, but AEMILIUS*). The honorand's name is picked out extra-large, in two self-contained lines; the dedicatee's name modestly features in medium size, as a 'second paragraph'. The whole message occupies the available field with military efficiency; the word-groups for each line have been planned accurately and without mistakes, each line 'centred' in its own right.

There is craft and skill in the emphatic repetitions that pull out the distinguished military record, from the first post as 'military tribune of the Thirteenth legion', emphasized by its mid-way size between the name and the rest of the roll-call. Once a legionary, always a legionary: for Roman veterans regularly retired together, kept a club membership for life, and stayed in touch with former comrades across the world.[34] How much Gallicus' affiliation to either of 'his' legions counted for through the rest of his life, and in his thoughts and attachments, is for us to estimate. They may have been the making of him. The stone-cutter brings out the double affiliation by matching the pairs *LEG XIII / GEMINAE* and *LEG XV / APOLLINARIS*. Further dominating the list of civvy magistracies are the pair */ LEGATO . . . LEGATO /*, which help to bring out the syntactical structure that binds the whole message into one unit, completed in the pregnant final word: *LEGATO /*.

This parting shot scatters our scholarship:

[1] It may be that we are just being told that Aemilius' dedication is on behalf of troops loyal to their *former legate in Galatia*, as

(a)

(b)

(c)   (d)

Figure 2(a)–(d). The Rutilius Gallicus inscription *in situ* at Ephesus:
photographs courtesy of Dr Hans Taeuber.

displayed a couple of lines above.[35] If there is special reason for the dedication in Ephesus, we need only presume that the troops returning home, or re-stationed, stopped long enough to leave their mark on the embarcation port, on hearing on the grapevine of his coming elevation to the consulate.

[2] Alternatively, we could suppose that this spanking statue represents a dedication directly bound up with Ephesus and the province of Asia. Then the inscription will indicate, not Gallicus' past relations to those cohorts, but his *present* position as 'legate', *scil. of Asia*. The sphere of responsibility is taken as read, sufficiently glossed and blessed as the most recent tenure of an expert with two previous terms in analogous authority. The first position was hallowed by reference to imperial appointment; the second by specification of the region involved. If the inscription manages to emblazon the sanctifying legends 'Divinized Claudius' and 'priest of Augustus', it will still contrive to point unerringly to its own circumstances. For Gallicus must be an imperial appointee, a legate sent out by the same ruler that deified (his [adoptive] father) Claudius, namely Nero, great-grandson of Augustus, whose suicide left that gap filled by Gallicus' priesthood; and Gallicus has been sent out as (propraetorian) 'legate', assistant to the governor, of the prize senatorial province of Asia. Hence the 'immortalization' of Gallicus' life to date in the administrative centre of the province, *at Ephesus*. If operations of Legion *XV* on the Danube are left undefined, mention of the province of *Galatia* may *both* concern the citizens of Asia more closely *and* implicitly motivate Aemilius' decision or agreement to honour Gallicus. As we shall see (chapter 2), Statius specially thrusts forward Gallicus' magnetism *for Asia* (or *vice versa*), and we are bound to try our hardest to fit paper to stone.

However that may be, the stone comes to a climax in its last line in the list of Gallicus' honours: *CONSULI DESIGNATO* / (rhyming with *LEGATO* /, three lines above, and *LEGATO* /, three lines below). When we look up (literally and metaphorically) to Gallicus in stone, we passers-by are supposed to see in this imperial legate 'next year's consul', a trajectory beyond what the statue could show, a promise of a route upwards for the officers of Rome. To be sure, the legions knew in 70 exactly how important they were for upward social mobility, including the throne. They had been the making of Vespasian, first generalissimo to take Rome from the east. So staff-officers could look forward to aping their masters. Gallicus was doing so at once.

But this is a lot to hang on Statius' mannered verses and the inscription's pregnant silence. And Gallicus' statue *is* lost. What became of Ephesos, by contrast, is well attested: denied the privilege of hosting either the cities of Asia's joint imperial cult for Tiberius and Livia, or for Gaius, on the grounds, or pretext, that Artemis dominated her city, Ephesos found Domitian prepared to grant a massive temple complex with colossal statues for the Flavian family (in 89/90), consolidated by the foundation of 'the Ephesian Olympics' (*c.* 90).[36] Very shortly, the bubble burst, when the masons enjoyed a brief boom as they were put to removing *Domitianus . . . Germanicus* from so many public monuments (see chapter 4). There is no particular reason to suppose Gallicus' statue was brought down just four or five years after his death by the assassination of 'his' emperor; and on the other hand, it could be that his demolition in stone in some way actually helped his *inscription* survive to become part of the city's later defences.[37] Which medium gave the best chances of perpetuity? For Gallicus, off to, or at, Rome as consul, then *LEGATUS* once more, in Africa, and in charge of province Asia a decade after Aemilius' dedication, it has proved a close-run thing—on paper *or* in stone.

2

Coordinates for a C. V.

Augustan poetry, above all late Horatian lyric, had devised a by turns asyndetonic (no connectives) or polysyndetonic (crawling with 'and's) style of 'epigraphic poetry' that cultivated 'the general paratactic austerity and brevity, typical of [inscriptional *elogia*]', trading 'prosiness' for formal authority and daring to frame Roman glory even in ultra-Hellenizing lyric stanzas.[38] Working to and fro between the Ephesus inscription and Statius' effusion can show us a lively associative imagination capitalizing on the latent potential of the career inscription to suggest characterful traits of self-representation. *Siluae* 1. 4 reads out Gallicus' path toward membership of the élite of Rome from the condensed materials assembled in his *cursus*. You should expect a Gallicus to have had someone to do his briefings for him, though he did very likely have Statius round for a dinner or two (a binge? an orgy?).

As an entrée to further scrutiny of Domitian's Rome through the experience of Gallicus, I am going to propose (more or less skittishly, mind) a string of a baker's dozen (or so) verbal-conceptual notions that Statius takes from the lineaments of Gallicus' public identity and turns into compliments for his intimates. There will be opportunity enough to come back to any of the details gathered here, when the poem gets the full treatment; for now, the idea is to feel how meaning gets unpacked and released from the dull stuff of names, referentiality, and chronological sequence.

[1] Gallicus is son of *Secundus* ('Follower/Favourable').
    That must be why papa 'was *second-best* and glad to yield his place', vv. 69f., *luce* sequente *uincitur et . . . gaudet cessisse*, 'as the brightness *succeeded* him'.

16

[2] Gallicus was made a *Iulius*.

Hence a scion of Troy, like Rome itself, like every 'Caesar' (v. 55), like an Augustus (e.g. holding saecular games; bridging the Araxes, v. 79; or triumphantly receiving a crushed world, vv. 89f.). And a 'Trojan', too, like Asklepios' Pergamum (*Troiana . . . Pergamus*, vv. 99f.), like Virgil's epic—and Horace's saecular—Aeneas (vv. 101f.), like the *Troica . . . saecula* of Priam/Tithonus/Sibyl (vv. 125f.).[39]

[3] Gallicus became *Cordinus*, son of *Cordus*.

This is why Statius plunges in to proclaim him Captain 'Darling', '*cordially*' binding heaven to gods, (to) emperor to minister, (to) Gaul to German, with heart-strings': *Gallicus. es caelo, dis es, Germanice,* cordi, v. 4.

[4] He did '*star*' in the tribe *Stellatina* (the right tribe for citizens from Turin).

Gallicus was presumably a firmament favourite in his civilized friend *Stella*'s circle of poetastra. The poem positively twinkles like an orrery: *Astraea . . . sidera, astris / luna, . . . luce . . ., clarus . . ., sole . . ., sidera . . . luce . . . nocte . . . lumine . . ., candentia* ('Stellate; stars; stars and moon; light; bright; sun; stars; light and night; light in the eyes; shining bright', vv. 2f., 36f., 69, 71, 73, 117–19, 123). Can I just mention that *Rutilius* connotes 'gleam and dazzle', too?

[5] The name *Gallicus* ('Français') makes him just the henchman for that other auld enemy of Rome, *Germanicus* ('Deutschisch', v. 4).

More, destiny nominated to challenge and provoke this *legatus / prouinciae Galaticae /* (so prominently stressed in the inscription for *Gallico /*) the raiding violators of Apollo's Delphi and of Asklepios' and Rome's Pergamum, the Gallic/Celtic hordes all the way from 'Galatea' (vv. 76f, 99f.).

[6] Gallicus served the Legion named *Gemina* ('Twin/Double').

So no wonder, *whatever* Statius may be talking up here, that he won 'twin tenures of office and repeat judicial rights over Asia' (geminos *fasces iterataque . . . / iura Asiae,* vv. 80f., cf. *ter . . . quaterque . . . reuocant fasti . . . nec semel,* 'three times and four; but recall by the clock that makes Rome tick; not just once', vv. 80–3). This must gild the lily of Gallicus' double, his second,

17

consulate, which Apollo *surely* could not obliviate—whether or not *also* embracing the praetorship, and/or the disputed spell as legate in Asia; whether or not Statius' phrases both concern *Asia*; whether the first, or conceivably both, refer to a prorogation over two years of his governorship of Asia in the early 80s, before his summons to return for the second consulate (82/3 and 83/4; 85).

[7] Gallicus had once served in the metropolis as *curulis aedilis*.
That was before he 'rose to a still higher throne'—presumably the consulship (*maiorque* curulis, v. 82).

[8] This veteran could be proud and gratified to find his (other) regiment, the *legio XV Apollinaris*, on parade as providing the entire figuration of his *poem*.
Apollo is first the *Phoebus* sidelined by Gallicus' strong poetry (vv. 19ff.), then the eponymous power within the 'groves blessed with Apollo's name' (*Apollineos sancto cognomine lucos*, v. 59); honoured with saecular worship and song (vv. 17f., 96f.), Apollo honours Gallicus with care and cure, with the spell of his singing (vv. 60–111); he is the Trojan/Roman god of poets like Gallicus, Statius and Stella (v. 117) and he keeps the Empire safe, through his priestess Sibyls (v. 126) and through the likes of Arruntius Stella, the priestly board of *xv uiri s[acris] f[aciundis]* who ward the books of oracular revelation.

[9] Duties in *Africa*.
This policing makes of Gallicus, not one of Vespasian's mean extortionists, but a sort of new-fangled 'Fabius', defender of Italy against Hannibal's Alpine invasion, plus an avenging 'Scipio', with no need to exact Regulus' gleeful revenge for the First Punic War (vv. 83–8).

[10] Poetry, as we are here defining it, almost *demanded* that he see service in *Germany*.
Working for his Roman chief *Germanicus*. And proving the answer to all the Joan of Arc-prophetess-from-the-Black Forest's prayers (vv. 89–91).

[11] In *Asia*.
Governor Gallicus really did run Pergamum, Thymbra and the Troad (vv. 81, 100, 117, 125).

[12] But at his acme, the double *consularis* Gallicus suffers and recovers as *Praefectus Urbi*.

His poem defends the inevitability of this, as we shall propose, from its first, and to the last, breath. The customary route to this office is summed up like this: 'arrive through a portfolio of credits to a repeat consulate, and then prefecture of Rome' (*qui per honores diuersos ad secundum consulatum et praefectum urbis peruenit, Scriptores Hist. Aug. Pius*, 1. 2). As we noticed, appointees were for life: so guarding Rome became a *Vita*.

[13] But if this is your life, Gallicus, nevertheless, Statius' flaunting text represses, or at least disguises, what may be its single most binding principle: Gallicus' home-town is *not* mentioned by name.

These verses, however, are studded with kindred notions: esp. *nec origo latet*, 'and the source is no secret', v. 69, cf. *alumnum*, 'fosterling', v. 21, *alumni*, 'fosterling', v. 60, *tecta*, 'roof', v. 63, *domos*, 'homes', v. 73; and *urbes*, 'cities', v. 11, *Epidauria proles*, 'offspring from Epidaurus', v. 61, *pater . . . Thymbraee*, 'father from Thymbra', v. 117. We shouldn't, then, give up too soon on Gallicus' origins.

The region—at least the region whence Apollo launched his Alpine rescue mission for to save Gallicus, no longer 'careless of his mighty fosterling' (*tanti . . . securus alumni*, v. 60)—is signposted clearly enough as 'sacred forest, high up on the roof-ridge of the world and known by the Alpine/Apolline signature' (*Alpini qui iuxta culmina dorsi / signat Apollineos sancto cognomine lucos*, vv. 58f.). Hints abound, of towering heights, cf. *sublimis*, 'elevated', v. 35, *alta*, 'high', v. 44, *tecta*, 'roof', v. 67, *transcendere*, 'o'erpass', v. 126. Since *Alpes* were so-called because either 'Sabines dub white alpish' or else 'the name [was] taken from the whiteness of the snow' (*album . . . Sabini alpum dixerunt*; *nomen Alpium a candore niuium uocitatum*, Paul. Fest. 4), they colour the various bright lights through the text, and above all the final flourish of 'snow-white bulls' (*niueos . . . tauros*, v. 129). But *Alpes* also, more pointedly still, 'in ancient Gallic spell apexes at altitude' (*Gallorum lingua alti montes uocantur*', Serv. *Aen*. 4. 442).[40]

Now the Celtic word *taur* for 'tor' gave its name to the Piedmontese tribal homeland of the *Taurini*.[41] Romanized sub-Alpines could only welcome this chance of language which made their folk the mighty mountain chain protecting/menacing Italy and at once 'Raging Bulls' to a man (*taurini*): the proudest, malest, largest thing on legs, and so the incarnate valuation placed by Romans on their Almighty *Iuppiter Optimus Maximus* every time that their triumphs offered up hecatomb sacrifices of victims marked with the dazzling white hides of an Alpine avalanche: *tauros* (vv. 128f.).

Connection between Gallicus' tribal homeland at *Augusta Taurinorum* and 'Alpine Apollo' might conceivably mark the local splendour of some temple sited in *Regio VIII, Aemilia*, on Augustus' map of Italy, as the humanist Politian (with customary polish) suggested long ago, with reference to Mart. 10. 12. 1, 'The peoples of *Regio VIII*: for a start, Apollo's Vercellae . . .' (*Aemiliae gentes et Apollineas Vercellas . . .*).[42] But far more potent connections bind Rutilius Gallicus' Turin to Domitianus Augustus Germanicus' Rome in the figure of Apollo. On the presumption that Rutilius cared about his roots, let us belabour the point, and see where it gets us.

Firstly, the *domus Flauia* was obliged, or given the opportunity, to restore the colony of Turin, severely burned by fire in the Civil War that founded the dynasty,[43] and likewise to restore the Palatine temple of Apollo, severely damaged in the Great Fire of 80: 'May the Palatine despise the flames and rise anew' (1. 1. 34). By 92 the massive palace complex, *domus Palatina*, was complete.[44] Domitian must also 'restore' a gutted 'Capitol', another casualty of the Fire of 80 (*quod reddis Capitolium*, 1. 6. 102: last line of the book). Thus the six-poem set of *Siluae* I sings a song of Domitianic renewal of Eternal Rome. His courtiers get caught up in the mood: there is Stella's re-marriage (1. 2); Vopiscus' villa for re-creation (1. 3); and Claudius Etruscus' refreshingly futuristic designer-sauna (1. 5). The revival *of Gallicus* knits all this onto the emperor's celebration of the saecular games, whose choir sang Rome into the piously reverential shape, from Apollo's Palatine through Forum to Jupiter's Capitol, of Domitian's Renaissance (Figure 3).

Secondly, and more compellingly, as we shall see in chapter 7, the Sibylline saecular song-and-dance hailed (Palatine) Apollo as 'Founder'.[45] Augustus' temple dedication on 9 October 28 B. C. E. of Apollo *Palatinus* would be celebrated forever more as a principal founding moment in the establishment of the

Figure 3. Coin with bust of Domitian and scene from his saecular games (*BMCRE* II. 425).

Principate—the entire apparatus of Graeco-Roman power installed in one flagship complex.[46] T/Here, the great sculptor Skopas' looted *Apollo of Delphi* played the lyre-strings that can turn in an instant to the twanging bow-string of the archer god of war, of plague ('the god who killed Python in person plays songs in sweeping robes', Prop. 2. 31. 16, *deus ipse . . . / Pythius in longa carmina ueste sonat*, cf. 'you played songs for me (Apollo) in noble purple', vv. 96f., *mihi . . . carmina patricio . . . sonuistis in ostro*[47]). And twin temple-doors imaged, in carved ivory, 'the Gauls driven back from the heights of Delphi' (*deiectos Parnasi uertice Gallos*', Prop. 2. 31. 13). This, Apollo's victory over those hybristic (third century BCE) invaders the Celtic 'Galatians', as proclaimed to the world by the sculptures of the Great Altar of Pergamum, would be repeated once more in the rout of the Galatians by Apollo's protégé Gallicus (vv. 76f.). And what is any of this to Turin? Well, the '*Colonia Iulia Augusta Taurinorum*' was one of the 'at most four towns in Italy' which 'were "new towns" on virgin sites' among 'the colonies established between 47 and 14 BC . . . In each case the original site name has been suppressed.' Turin, like several towns which 'at a date unknown, but necessarily after 27 BC, . . . acquired the additional title Augusta [and so became] *Iulia Augusta*, . . . could well belong immediately after Actium . . . Augustus may have wished later to link more closely to his name certain colonies, perhaps the twenty-eight which he was to claim in the Res Gestae as his own foundations.'[48] So it is entirely *possible* that the entry into his name of 'Augustus' in 27 BCE was contemporaneous with *both* the foundation of Turin *and* the inauguration of Palatine Apollo. At any rate, at some point in the history of Turin between 28 BCE and 1416 [*sic*], the strongest of links between these two originary moments was built into, if not the fabric, then at least the *nomination* of the colony, whose northern gate towering over its Augustan city-walls claims the title of '*Porta* Palatina' to this day (Figure 4).[49] And indeed one of the two inscriptions which attest *C. Rutilius Gallicus cos. II* was even 'excavated in 1801 at Turin in taking down the Palatine Gate' (*Taurinis effossa a. 1801 in demolitione portae Palatinae*, CIL 5. 6988, *ad loc.=ILS* 1007). 'The extravagant and menacing towers have a primarily symbolic character, since the gate itself was not secured by the corresponding defensive installations.'[50]

Figure 4. 'Palatine Gate', Turin (model in the Museo della Civiltà Romana, Rome, *INR* 73. 944).

Thirdly, and more briefly, the three-day Great Fire of Rome in 80 brought with it 'plague—the measure of which isn't easily paralleled' (*pestilentia quanta non temere alias* . . ., Suet. *Tit.* 8. 3).[51] Linkage between the celebration of the saecular games and Gallicus' recovery from near-fatal illness *may* be the axis around which Statius turns Domitian's revival of burned and ailing Rome.[52]

[14] As a still more speculative coda, we might attend to the priestly boasts in Gallicus' *cursus*: *pontifex* and *sodalis Augustalis* (and make this the final point).

Quite shrouded in the antiquity of Turin is the local cult lurking behind the inscription from a herm-base at Turin, which *might* even tie Gallicus' *soteria* to his *patria*:

D i u o T r a i a n [o]

C . Q u i n c t i u s
A b a s c a n t u s
test[amento]   leg[auit]
m e d i c i s   T a u r [i n i s]
C u l t o r [i b u s
A s c l e p i   e t
H   y   g   i   a   e
(ILS 3855a)[53]

To: The Immortalised Trajan.

From: C. Quinctius
A b a s c a n t u s
by testamentary bequest
to the Doctors of Turin,
the worshippers of Asclepius and
H y g i [e i] a .

Was Gallicus one of these faithful, back home?

3

Playing Second Fiddle

The poet's Gallicus will prove to be like 'the illusory towers' of some tauriform 'Palatine' Gate to an Augustan fortress, posed as if 'defender of city and world', *custos urbis / orbis*. The Prefect figures an omnipresent, world-straddling rôle, from the Alpine passes of Piedmont's Turin to the walled hills of Rome, from Apollo's Delphi to Asklepios' Epidauros and the towers of Pergamum. Warden of Fortress Empire (see Figures 5a, b and c). Now is the moment to assess the force of this fancy, against the soup of politics in the tureen of Flavian history. What was it to be Domitian's Urban Chief?

'La préfecture de la Ville . . . devait l'élever au rang de second personnage de l'Empire.'[54] This illusory post, its Republican aura as bogus as Gallicus', could be considered the 'true apex of the senatorial career': 'The post was, arguably, the most important after the emperor himself.'[55] In fact the post was one important arena in which to play emperor. One way to shape and evoke autocratic power is always to model modes of subordination around relations with 'deuteragonists': know all monarchs in their policing, vilifying and celebrating of caretakers and deputies, right-hand-men and next-in-line, all those-most-likely to . . .

Roman versions of this drama of power were rehearsed even before the start of the Principate: '(Maecenas) was at this time [the late 30s BCE] 'the second most powerful man in Rome; yet he remained an elusive and enigmatic figure, a *priuatus* and an *eques* whose power resided in his *amicitia* with Octavian.'[56] And in the red corner, Agrippa, '(the victorious party's) greatest general, and admiral . . . Even in the

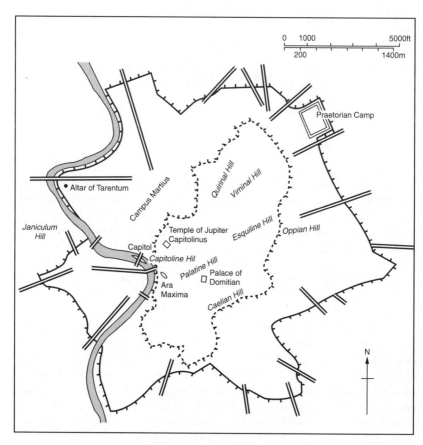

Figure 5a. The city of Rome.

twenties, he was unquestionably the second man in Rome', 'Marcus Vipsanius Agrippa, . . . up to the time of his death in 12 BC was the number two man in Rome', 'Agrippa as *adiutor imperii*, the almost mythical model for a right-hand man of the emperor'.[57] The duet of Augustus and Agrippa, as they led the prayers and made the saecular offerings in 17 BCE, was especially recalled in the tableau which Domitian's 'recent' resumption, on the Augustan calculation (or near as makes no odds), must have taken for its inspiration or anxiety of influence.[58] We don't know either way, but *perhaps* the Prefect of the City had been privileged as *his* Augustus' deuteragonist in 88? Rutilius Gallicus, then, could have *seemed* 'a powerful man in the state, second only to the emperor', or he could have *been* 'second in power only to the emperor himself', as Statius makes clear when he calls him 'the closest of necks' (*proxima ceruix*, v. 6).[59] Thus Juvenal will have Pegasus land as *praefectus Urbi* first, so arguably foremost, in his list of arrivals for Domitian's cabinet.[60]

It wouldn't have been a bad bet to back this job of City Manager as potential springboard to the highest ambition of all: the next known Prefect of the City after Gallicus was T. Aurelius Fuluus, legate of *Legio III Gallica*, who prosecuted Vespasian's cause in 69, was *cos.* 70, *cos. II ord.* in 85; *his* grandson did indeed turn purple as the emperor Antoninus Pius.[61] And Vespasian's own elder brother, Flavius Sabinus, had been Nero's City Prefect all the way from 56 through 68: dismissed by Galba, reinstated by his cohorts under Otho, retained by Vitellius while his cohorts were replaced by German legionaries, Sabinus protected the adolescent princeling Domitian in the enemy capital Rome and attempted, finally, to lever Vitellius into abdication and survival in the Temple of Apollo, only for the praetorians to eliminate the negotiator and throw his body in the Tiber. Such was the Flavians' first real bow to the royal box.[62] Domitian could easily have been over-impressed with the scope rather than the limitations of the post.

Gallicus' own breakthrough may have come when as *sodalis Augustalis* he stepped into Nero's dead man's shoes in 68/9. It could be possible to detect in the Chief Constable aspirations more easily associated with the Praetorian Prefect, especially after the negative paradigm of Sejanus, Tiberius' trusted 'Partner of my Labours'.[63] Paranoid or prudent suspicion could unfold *Gallicus'* 'home-town, character, and the crime that was his path toward seizing the throne'— did *he* 'oblige' *his* Caesar 'with a spectrum of strategies'? (Tac. *Ann.* 4. 1) Like wicked Sejanus, Gallicus' 'body had a high capacity for labour, a

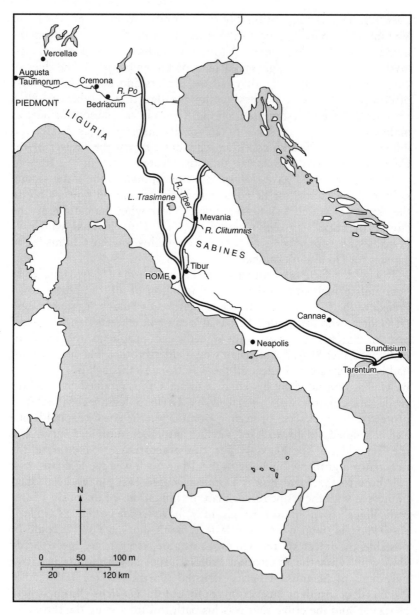

Figure 5b. Italy.

bold mind, most times out of ten effort round the clock' (ibid.), and he too could point to his *cursus* and boast 'He had never requested any attractive appointment . . . but preferred to work to preserve his imperial C.-in-C. with the night-watch and labours of an ordinary soldier' (ibid. 39. 2). To complete the circle, of lieutenants circling all too closely round the throne: 'The obvious analogy is Augustus' great minister Maecenas, who never sought political advancement but remained an *eques* throughout his life' and Sejanus 'perhaps deriv[ed] this element of his image [as an ideal general] from Augustus' other great minister, the soldier Agrippa, an archetypal man of labor'.[64] As 'emperor's assistant—and how much further before he was called his colleague in office!' (ibid. 4. 7. 2)—Rutilius Gallicus could, with the appropriate disclaimers and obliquity, well find himself Rome's deuteragonist. And, if not for real, he could walk the part in anyone's diagram of power.

To be sure, there is nothing to say each City Prefect wasn't out-ranked by every 'Maecenas' (Petronius, Seneca, . . .), out-gunned by all the battle-scarred 'Agrippas' (Marius, Corbulo, Agricola . . .), out-strutted by each Praetorian 'Sejanus' (Macro, Burrus, Tigellinus, Mucianus . . .). We shall see what Statius' Apollo can talk Gallicus' record up to, on paper (chapter 14). Maybe the City job was, beyond a venture, just a sedentary sinecure: 'The office demanded discretion, and complaisance, not without a gift for intrigue'.[65] Burrus, for instance, surely saw mostly paper legions, though (most crucial) he certainly looked the part—'a terrific fighting reputation, . . . all military solutions to military problems and stiff morals, . . . missing one hand but still demanding to rule the human race'![66] Imperial Rome kept the old polarity between 'Home' and 'Military' spheres, together with its pomp and imagery, though under normal conditions the latter essentially covered 'provincial admin.' and 'government'.[67] In that case, it is merely a chance that Gallicus attracted his one (extended) poetic treatment, whereas, for example, the bare name of the bullish Augustan *cos. suff.* 37, *cos. II* 26 BCE and *praefectus urbi* 18/16–13 (or later) BCE, T. Statilius Taurus, features in the poetry of his era just the once—and then purely as the date of a vintage.[68] Statius could be making something of a 'Maecenas' of Gallicus not least to match Horatian lyric, where the Grand Old Man was forever care-worn.[69] In any case, the anonymous elegiac portrait of Maecenas is the best preparation for Statius' Gallicus you could wish for (*Elegy for Maecenas* 12f., 16, 23, 27, 31, 136, 139):

Figure 5c. The Roman Empire.

tu Caesaris almi / dextera, Romanae tu uigil urbis eras; te sensit nemo posse nocere tamen; sic illi uixere, quibus fuit aurea Virgo / quae . . . pulsa fugit; num minus urbis erat custos et Caesaris obses?; maius erat potuisse tamen nec uelle triumphos; te sumus obliti decubuisse senem; Nestoris annosi uicisses saecula.

You were the right hand of kind Caesar, you were the City Watch of Rome; no one ever felt that you could do harm; such was life when golden Astraea was on earth, before she was pushed and fled; was he not the City's Guard and Caesar's Bulwark?; a greater achievement to have triumphs in the hand only to refuse them; we forgot you passed away past your prime; you'd have beaten the aeons of age-old Nestor.

Perhaps, for all that Domitian had married a daughter of Corbulo, Domitia, the looming figure of the 'Domitius big enough to fill the shoes of a Trajan', 'clearly a menace to Nero',[70] perhaps the disciplinarian soldier-hero and imperial victim Domitius Corbulo always hovered above Gallicus, his former legionary legate in the east—alongside that model for a soldier-emperor, the elder Trajan; and alongside Aurelius Fuluus, too, as we saw, himself another *cos. II* of 85 and another future City Prefect, and one with imperial loins.[71] Possibly Rutilius Gallicus' career even cloned in the illustrious career of the other senator from Turin, Q. Glitius Atilius Agricola, *cos II* and Urban Prefect sometime between 103 and 117.[72] More crucially, Gallicus' rise shadowed his predecessor's with ominous contiguity: M. Arrecinus Clemens *cos.* 73, *cos. II* 85, and *praefectus urbi c.* 84–7 (?).[73] For gentle Clemens had been executed by Domitian (Suet. *Dom.* 11. 2).

A rapidfire narrative of the crises facing Domitian and his Prefect and this book is through with history. After the next chapter, it will be poetry the whole way, remember:

> *Wie man in den Wald hineinruft, so schallt's heraus.*
> The sound that comes out of the *Siluae* depends on the noise you
> put into them.[74]

4

Sand-bagging the Danube

These *Siluae* trace a profile for the middle years of Domitian's reign. Book I preserves a considered review of the late 80s and early 90s. 1. 4's passing moment of Gallicus' short-lived recovery from illness is buttoned to grand Roman history through two explicit markers:

[1] 'Your career's recent zenith: Rome entrusted to you during the massacre of Dacians' (vv. 90f., *quae maxima nuper gloria, / depositam Dacis pereuntibus urbem*).

[2] 'Boys, you recently chanted my song of praise' (vv. 96f., *mihi nuper honora / carmina . . ., pueri, sonuistis*).

The coordinates, then, are these: the saecular games of September 88; and (as we could put it) Domitian's double triumph over Dacians and Chatti in November 89, celebrating Tettius Iulianus' 'great battle and . . . great slaughter of Dacians' at Tapae in autumn 88.[75] Rutilius Gallicus' Prefecture of the City, the summation of his career, is interset with these larger themes.

'One entire legion, probably V *Alauda*, was lost in the fatal campaign of AD 8[6].'[76] The Praetorian Prefect Cornelius Fuscus lost army and life in a reprisal raid into Dacia. On 22 September 87, the Arval Brotherhood sacrificed in Rome 'In thanks for the detection of terrorist wickedness' (*CIL* 6. 2065, *ob detecta scelera nefariorum*). Probably this refers to the elimination of M. Arrecinus Clemens, 'founder-member' of the Flavian dynasty, Titus' in-law and a personal agent of Domitian, executed for conspiracy.[77] This is how Rutilius Gallicus unexpectedly

33

found himself handed the plum job, or poisoned chalice. Was he looking forward to a settled old age in post?

As we have seen, Domitian looked among the double consulars and found Gallicus, as he would be obliged to look again, much sooner than contemplated, within just four or five years, among the magistrates of the unruffled year 85 (i.e. the likes of both Arrecinus Clemens and Aurelius Fuluus). Security clearance for the new appointment will have found the profile of the long-term Flavian stalwart that we have pieced together. The trusted officer of Corbulo, with roots in two of the favourite Flavian legions, both currently engaged in the critical theatre of post-débâcle Dacia. With a world of experience, on Rhine and Danube, in Africa and Asia, the range of administration in Rome. Versatility, from responsibility for supply-line back-up to a dangerous war-zone (Galatia), to running a census operation (Africa), and to governing the richest province of all (Asia). Not the least consideration, it could be, this was a self-made success-story from nowhere, without a powerful local lobby or cabal and so entirely the emperor's creature (how much could Turin and Piedmont count at court?).

The saecular games of 88 may have been accelerated from a literal to a plausible Augustan calculation[78] in order to purge the body politic of the poison of conspiracy at home and, especially, military catastrophe abroad. As the last chapter speculated, the City Prefect may have taken a prominent, even co-starring, rôle in the pageant. For the new year of 89, Domitian may have broken his run of consulates as token of the security of the new *saeculum* (*coss. VIII–XIV* in 82, 83, 84, 85, 86, 87, 88).[79]

The further good news, of recovery on the Dacian front, will at once have been ruined by a new threat, a combination of conspiracy, barbarian invasion, and full-scale Civil War. Instead of decreeing new year wishes for the health of the emperor in the name of his two legions doubling-up at Moguntiacum in Upper Germany, the governor L. Antonius Saturninus (originally adlected to the senate by Vespasian and perhaps governor in the trouble spot of Judaea *c.* 78–81) spent 1 January 89 initiating a mutiny, or worse, thus repudiating Domitian's new age.[80] Saturninus probably also had the forces of the Chatti nation gather ready for a support invasion of the Empire (as they had tried before, in the Roman crisis of 69, along with the Dacians) in revenge for the defeats suffered earlier in the 80s. Meantime the Parthians threatened support for a 'false Nero' pretender and chaos in the east. Here was the real test of Domitian's nerve, and capability.

'Domitian displayed decision himself and expected it of others. Summoning, before it was too late, the Spanish legion VII *Gemina*, which its commander Trajan conducted with dutiful rapidity towards the seat of war, Domitian hastened with the Guard to northern Italy, there to concentrate his troops and, if necessary, fall back upon the Danubian armies. . . . By the twelfth day of the month (so acting on a tip-off) Domitian was on his way north; on the twenty-fifth the tidings of victory . . . were celebrated by the Arval brethren.'[81] The governor of Lower Germany, [A. Bucinus] Lappius Maximus, had crushed the rising, whatever its ambitions may have been, leaving the *Caesar Augustus* victorious over another, lesser, *Antonius*, as if in a repeat of Actium.[82]

After reprisals on both mutineers and Germans, Domitian headed on to reach Pannonia in spring 89, and eventually concluded terms with the Dacian 'Geronimo' King Decebalus, with a showpiece of 'vicarious homage' as a Dacian prince 'received a diadem from the hands of Domitian'.[83]

Back in Rome, the City Prefect Gallicus had been left as, at least in some sense, the emperor's deputy, while Domitian forced-marched up past Turin and over Apollo's Alps. The symbolic value of a warden called 'Gallicus' from a fortress founded by the first Augustus against just such an eventuality as invasion of Italy from the north must have come home to friends, Romans and countrymen. And the reality of the City Prefect's *custodia* must have become insistent when the Praetorian Prefects and Guard marched north with the emperor to face the tumult in defence of Rome, leaving just Gallicus and his cohorts to man the capital.[84] But Gallicus' finest hour, his fifteen minutes of fame, must have come when he had opened the gates, no doubt in person, for the triumphal entry in fall 89 for '*Germanicus*'', declared victories *de Germanis et Dacis*.[85] Perhaps Statius has his Apollo all-but mention 'the hordes from the frozen north; Rhine back on the warpath; the prayers of captive Veleda' (vv. 89f.), immediately before the climax to the 'Dacian massacre' (v. 91), so as to glance at the 'recent' threat from the Chatti.[86] The topic of Saturninus' 'civil crime' (*Silu.* 1. 1. 80, *ciuile nefas*) does not in so many words obtrude on 1. 4's prayerful scene of thanksgiving. But Gallicus' recovery very likely coincided with Rome's.

One development from the multiple threats of the 'recent' past may have been to persuade Domitian to name the sons of his cousin Flavius Clemens and Domitilla his heirs 'Vespasian' and 'Domitian', in 90 or soon after.[87] But, perhaps like the 'plague' that seems to have afflicted at least the Rome élite in the years after the saecular games,[88] the body politic was not to heal, and Gallicus' death only prevented him seeing the deterioration of Rome that would find, three years after the end of his Prefecture, the execution of both Praetorian Prefects and of Flavius Clemens (in 95), the elimination of rows of courtier-senators leading ultimately to that of the *pater urbis* himself, Domitian, and the end of the dynasty (in 96). As Statius stopped publishing, and writing, *Siluae*, and stopped breathing, the Flavians were becoming a re-run of Pindar's fraternal Sicilian tyranny, where good Gelon gives way to problematic Hieron, before non-credible Thrasybulus fouls up: 'Within a year of Hieron's death, the rule of the Deinomenids in Sicily had ended forever.'[89]

Back in Rome, imbrication and repulsion between soldiers and civilians were equally insistent in the contest to control the World State. Could all the Gallicuses reconcile their disengaged selves? Could they bring partnership, or hierarchy, to these twin profiles? Could their Flavian dynasty dovetail these cultural identitities? Would the socialites forget what the soldiers had proved in 69? Would the armies' interests detach from those of central government? Statius will rough out some thoughts on this through his Gallicus.

5

Thank Heaven for That:
vv. 1–8

si canimus siluas, siluae sint consule dignae
If *Siluae* are our song, let them deserve a consul.

Virgil, *Eclogue* 4. 3

Estis, io, superi, nec inexorabile Clotho
uoluit opus. uidet alma pios Astraea Iouique
conciliata redit, dubitataque sidera cernit
Gallicus. es caelo, dis es, Germanice, cordi
(quis neget?): erubuit tanto spoliare ministro   5
imperium Fortuna tuum. stat proxima ceruix
ponderis immensi damnosaque fila senectae
exuit atque alios melior reuirescit in annos.

You are there, yea, gods above, and this side of inexorability Fate
    Clotho
whirls her spinning work! Motherly Astraea looks upon the
    godfearing, and reconciled
with Jove she returns, and there gazes, too, upon the stars feared lost
Gallicus! You have heaven's heart, Germanicus, you have the gods'!
Who would deny it? Too embarrassed to strip the great servant from   5
your empire—that's Lady Luck! Stands right by your side, head
    unbowed
by the infinite burden, and old age's threads laden with loss
he sloughs, and finds himself growing young again, his better years
    up ahead!

In Statius' hands, Gallicus's story maps Roman culture, with the accent on the softer interiors of Roman City life: the seven hills, saecular games, courts, a caring administration and miracle cure, the man of letters and the Hellenized courtiers. In this vision, Statius plays the conductor who inducts reader-citizens to his choir. Energized by a whole store of deeply imprinted icons of civic sentiment, his fancy writing bids to connect the Rome we inhabit to a precarious world-order where the concord of collective harmony can work miracles. It will only work if we join in. What really happens in such a stunt, in the togetherness of any congregation, is that the will-power of a community calls into existence, affirms-and-naturalizes, a particular configuration of cultural hierarchy. It feels like sharing, in one accord, of your own accord. But when a congregation prays together, the people pool desire, invest in a longing, and commit themselves to cherish the truth of this experience. The priest speaks before, and (to get real) to, the flock, but the power of the collective will transfers this into speaking *for* the flock, on their behalf, as if crowds really lead, and pontiffs bring no agenda. Statius enlists his Roman readers to value his verses by playing the patriotic card. His lure to readers works like this: participate, and keep Rome safe, just sing along with the song, it's yours.[90]

A prominent civil servant/courtier leads the way as role-model for his society. He offers public service as the salvation of the state. Let every citizen embrace this in their own terms. In short, this minister's case serves to mediate, between humble mortals and supreme divinity, a social compact. In a word, Statius promulgates *cura*. His lesson is a reading of 'affection', 'diligence', 'administration', 'preservation' and 'recovery', or 'cure'. Everywhere we turn, we are shown hallowed traditions, institutions and titulature oriented around *cura*; from the particular moment of Gallicus' crisis to the entire apparatus of eternal Rome. This poem can dress up autocracy itself as 'loving anxiety' and 'fearful devotion': *cura*.[91]

Celebration of Gallicus in one of the relatively informal *Siluae*, 'mainly in private terms . . . except [for] the concern of the urban populace',[92] does not mean that Statius is playing safe—ducking politics and evading the issue. The whole point of the public medium of élite reading-culture is to focus and orient civic discourse around the modelling and re-modelling of power-relations at the social summit. Institutions such as poetry frame terms for peaceful coexistence and parameters for (in)subordination; they need not only lead and reconcile people to their place. That is why the politics of reading is so crucial for any community this side of civil strife.

Granted that acclamation, acclamation by the poet in the name of The People, does bring the power-structure into play, and does mean to. Statius' acclamation effects and authorizes a masking of the real contestants for power, and foists this authorization on 'the Roman people'—as if the palace and the poet actually stemmed from and faithfully served them. Yet the poem does not (nor could it) simply perform, mime, or enact its charismatic symphony by appointment to the crown. Patriotic, manicured nullity? Poetic, saving grace? Statius has an agenda, too. When we have read through the poem, we shall consider how, within its book-collection, 1. 4 speaks to a poetic which exceeds and contains it (chapters 19–20).

For the moment, let's just say that Gallicus' *soteria* does more than celebrate the reach that such occasional ephemera as the *Silvae* may contrive across and to the quick of the cultural ensemble. For within the tasteful privacy of Statius' book-roll, the grandeurs of the Empire fold back into a reflection on the undecidable ironies of writing. There we may at leisure ponder powerfully/powerlessly to ourselves how come it (and the rest of us) are so stuck between power and powerlessness. In that context, the case of Rutilius Gallicus will evoke reflection on poetry, a particular brand of poetry, frame for a special kind of political thinking. You see, the poet, too, invests and demands *cura*. Our cultural myth of Literature commits us to absorb through literary representation the truths in collective representations such as prayer, thanksgiving, religious festival and choral hymn. Reading accesses the workings of the cosmos, so reading is where cultural power is dispensed. Truly, reading saves the world; books are formative and normative, they make readers and make worlds: *cura*.[93] If the temporary recovery of a tyrant's Chief of Security seems an unpromisingly jejune programme for an effortless flight of poetastry, so much greater the congratulations in order if the challenge is met.

In *Siluae* 1. 4 Statius 'offers up vows that Rutilius Gallicus be restored to health, not without details about the life and career of that high personage'.[94]

Let the poem begin!

The poem begins with a bang!

The poet plays priest for us. His apostrophe to the gods shouts it from the roof-tops: faith vindicated, waverers trounced—there *is* a god, something cares (v. 1).[95] The opening outburst evokes communal affirmation. This is how the divine is performed in discourse; such asseveration of divinity takes its meaning from the context in social exchange:[96] the utterance is 'phatic' (opens communication), filled with annunciatory promise. Grammatically the 'Hosanna' is complete enough, but it prefaces an account of the relationship it indicates between *superi* ('gods above') and the sublunary inferiority of the celebrant(s). It works the way a 'Let us pray' formula does, occasioning an account of the occasion which calls it forth. Although the passage will confine itself to a list of neutral connectives or to none at all—five 'and's and four [blanks] in vv. 1–8—the opening salvo binds what follows to the work of accounting for, explaining, contextualizing, glossing the cry of faith restored. Statius has got us in the right mood—now he must say what we are here for, he'll tell us what we're in for.

First he *supplements* his exclamation: 'and Clotho whirls her spinning this side of inexorability' (vv. 1f.). Welcome to the Graeco-Roman tandem of imperial Rome: feel the super-eloquent prestige of Hellenizing rhetoric match the sub-articulate pride of the Roman ritual noise (*io*).[97] The polysyllabic and emphatic adjective, the encircling phrase-structure, the release of verbal energy in the turn of the verse-unit, all p(l)ump up the mythic clap-trap. The *litotes* 'not inexorable' opens up space within which faith can work: envisage intercessionary prayer, doubt over its efficacy; the edge of despair. Exorability is a *stake*: prayer is all about persuasion and rhetoric, about belief in utterance. So is acclamation of prayers heard, which ought not to depend on eloquence, or consist in the gift of the gab, but owes it to faith, to the seriousness of the petition, and to the gods, to be beautiful as we can make it. The same goes for the thanksgiving, which should affirm all this, and should make this its message, that human intercession, if it is put as well as it can be put, works. Statius isn't wasting his time, then. Nor are we, if we join him. And his poem isn't a pointless exercise, either. For Clotho is not *just* here as a ready-made cliché from Greek poetry. She *also* figures the textuality *of the poem*. Before us is 'a work' (*opus*), a work of art spun fine by a winsome writer. A piece primed to 'roll out' the grandiose carpet of an unexpectedly sublime story of gods and Fate, Rome and salvation. Clotho takes charge of this performance, threading Statius' eloquence with the force of epic amplification.[98]

The next lines further amplify the 'Praise-Be' with more mythic stuff, featuring the personification Virgin Justice. Her connection with the Fate(s) is only that they both belong to the short-hand of poetic décor.

She lets this thanksgiving prove that the sun does shine on the righteous, a pious thought piously affirming the general truth (or pietism) about the just deserts of piety. The miraculous moment negates what is negative in our world, traditionally troped as heavenly 'Astraea's withdrawal from the wicked face of the earth'.[99] Our poem is promising theodicy (justification of the ways of deity). Something here and now reverses demoralized mythological tradition, with its primal descent from the Saturnian pre-cultural unconscious into Olympian desecration and Iron Age fracture, where we come in. In good time, Statius will specify his celebration as investment in a 'new age' (v. 17): the coming of Domitian.

At the same time Statius' words draw (ominous) attention, in denial, to the pagan condition of polytheist difference within divinity, to the plurality inherent in those 'gods above'. The rest of the poem will narrate the 'healing' of the rift which its first phrases already declare to be achieved. The point is that the disjunctiveness within classical divinity opens up space in which to explore transcendence, for the rule and realm of Jupiter provide a common horizon for all the relations in the story of Gallicus, especially between minister and emperor, then Aesculapius and Apollo. Justice returns to witness human goodness regain'd; the return is brought about by the restored harmony with Jupiter that it attests. The faithful earn her regard for the new age of Domitian. We are here to sing our regard for her, to stand and be counted, for all to see under heaven. Our harmony is geared to the gods'. A universe of respect is breaking out, presided over by Omnipotence in league with Justice. That's the deal: but what is the application?

It arrives in a lively flip of sense. As we are reading on from Astraea's first two phrases, with the verb 'looks' first word in her sentence, and 'returns' at the break half way through the line, a third phase arrives, perfectly naturally, linked with a second 'and', and with the verb 'gazes' completing the sense at verse-end, we have no doubt that we are dealing with as neat a tricolon as you could wish to behold.[100] 'Astraea regards, too, the stars feared lost.' Presumably she doubted she would return to see the sky ever again. Perhaps these 'stars' stand for the Olympian 'gods above', trust in whom had been in jeopardy. In any case, a cosmic crisis . . . is over. But once we turn to start the next verse, we run right into: / Gallicus.

With the Prefect's shock appearance we need to re-read and collect our thoughts. It turns out we have just celebrated, as if we knew it all along, *his* continued existence. Caring divinity and destiny have been on *his* case. His Roman life is proof that Fate can be turned around, and Fair Fairness bring conciliation to the cosmos. The fear and doubt we thought was Astraea's was the moment of crisis when the world all but lost Gallicus. This is the cliff-hanger that is mimetically re-enacted in every reading of the lines there ever will be. It was the moment he, and/or we, as good as despaired of his ever seeing another night on this earth. When astronomical, astrological, astrographic stabilities threatened to buckle.[101] That was the ordeal of (his/our) faith in the heavens above. And this has been the closest thing that poetic play with the release of language across the groove of rhetoric can get toward fashioning continuity between the crumbling of mortal confidence in the gods, and the gods' own doubt in heaven. Astraea's vote of no confidence, her walk-out on the firmament, is over before we come in; Gallicus' doubts are behind him. If he could, Statius would skip us past the bad vibes before they can register . . .

So prayers can be heard, (if) the gods can find unity, doubts (can) give way to affirmation. Next Statius's words reconcile divine plurality *and* divine oneness, through shared warmth to the emperor: both 'heaven' and 'gods' care for Domitian (v. 4). Feel him dissolve all and any difference.[102] At the same time, the conceptual 'rhyme' between the names sharing this verse[103]—'Gallicus' and 'Germanicus'—links them as aptly named spirits of Roman civilization, through their inoculatory power to annul assaults from the barbarian otherness(es) of *Gaul and Germany*. Both are triumphal victory-names, taken as prophylactic 'spoils' from the defeated. As we saw, Gallicus' full name of *Iulius Cordinus* helps collapse divine being(s) into one wave of love for Domitian, tugging any *heart*-strings (*cor*). Such love can conquer all, sin and death, fear or doubt. Domitian gives the gods above the opportunity to care: apostrophe to him succeeds apostrophe to them (*estis ~ es*). Justice joins love, to cure Jupiter's hostility and save Gallicus. So let us pray some more.

In fact Statius insists some more on his expression of faith: 'Who would deny it?' (v. 5). Why hold us up? Surely those declarative indicatives 'You are . . . you are' left us in no doubt whatever? The challenge, to the unrepentant, the unconvinced, is traditional practice in the policing of congregations. The question challenges the demon of envy to respond. Ministers and worshippers cannot be too careful. But the question is rhetorical. We *make* it rhetorical by surviving the moment when the chasm yawns, and the prayers are just begging to be blighted by some noisome response. We pass swiftly on, to fresh acclamation, and even some clarification. Indeed this is exactly where Gallicus is picked out as our concern: 'so great a servant' (v. 5). Where we get our bearings.

First we face down the Wicked Fairy at our thanksgiving, that demon of demons, Fortune. *She* could not deny that the cosmos loves Domitian, could not say no to Domitian, 'was embarrassed out of getting rid of Gallicus' (v. 5). Take note, anyone else out to spoil the party: Gallicus *lives*. Rescued by prayer and the standing of his patron with the powers-that-be, he 'exists'—*stat* (v. 6)—and 'stands upright, head unbowed'.[104] Acclamation in triplicate directs congratulation piled on recovery toward a final affirmation of triumph: 'exists . . . sloughs . . . finds himself growing young'. Amen.

Yet this conclusion to the opening of the *soteria* cries out, too, for further supplementation—for the 'Wherefore, . . .', as it proves, of the next paragraph (v. 9, *ergo* . . .). For Gallicus has only a human 'neck', beneath an 'infinite burden', he is getting older, even if he is getting 'better', the very 'return', *re-*, of vigour cannot stop time, does not make 'the years' the same; and the temporality within the inceptive verb '*begins to* grow young', *-escit*, itself marks the rhetorical strain of Statius' and anyone's prayers.[105] To bind the future, we *can* only string along the hollow certainties of the present indicative. But, however pious, however sanguine, however triumphalist, prayers can never shake free of their precariousness. No, mortality and longing go hand in hand (we are all conation, not cognition). Notice that even the prolepsis (attempt to forestall objection, foreclosure of difference) spoke from outside the syntactic chain: *(quis neget?)*.[106] This (parathetic) voice irrupts from somewhere else, and imports a note perilously close to despair of prolepsis. The logic is that our thanksgiving *needs* a heretic outsider who won't be exorcised, go away, or be silenced. This voice is in the heads of us pious believers, standing for our wonder at theurgy, keeping open the gap faith must leap, and generating the need for further asseveration, renewed devotion, amplified prayer. There is always more to declare.

6

Dancing in the Streets:
vv. 9–14

ergo alacres quae signa colunt urbana cohortes
inque sinum quae saepe tuum fora turbida questum   10
confugiunt leges urbesque ubicumque togatae,
quae tua longinquis implorant iura querelis,
certent laetitia, nosterque ex ordine collis
confremat, et sileant peioris murmura famae.

Wherefore, platoons that look lively, tending the ensigns of Rome;
law after law that takes sanctuary in your arms, protesting   10
breaches of the peace, and the Roman towns wherever
that appeal for your arbitration in telegrammed disputes:
let them all compete in happiness, let our every hill in due sequence
roar in concert! And let mutterings from no-good gossip hold their
      peace!

'Wherefore', we are treated with a second instalment of amplificatory
preliminaries, shoring up the protestation as we go. Care for their
representative must occasion communality among the Roman populace.
A social simultaneity where the poem conjures up a voice. The
thanksgiving for Gallicus wants to cast itself as the serried prayers of
Rome—answered, it says, and answered in triplicate. Statius declares
that Rome is used to addressing all its appeals, petitions and pleas to
Prefect Gallicus, 'platoons that . . .; laws that . . .; towns that . . .' (vv.
9–14, *quae . . . cohortes*; . . . *quae . . . leges*; *urbes . . . quae*):

44

[1] The City's whole garrison 'jumps' at Gallicus' commands; these soldiers 'worship' their C.-in-C., the *Praefectus Urbi*, and all he stands for, 'every Latin word, the divinity of his Roman ensigns' (v. 9).

[2] The entire judicial apparatus depends on the 'sanctuary the High Judge's bosom offered Law, on all the occasions when breaches of the peace disturbed due process' (vv. 10f.).

[3] The length and breadth of Italy, 'every city where togas are worn turns to The City, begging justice from Gallicus in their far-off disputes' (vv. 11f.).[107]

This civil servant services his world, you see, answers every prayer, everywhere. This is his routine, his duty, his Roman life. Statius masses in four verses the round of continuous appeal to Gallicus that constituted his office, mimetically realized in the rhythms of his writing. He parades concentric word-patterning: *alacre*s . . . *sig*na c*olunt urba*na c*ohortes* / (v. 9); interwoven rhythms of sound: / inque sinum quae sae*pe* tuum *fora* tu*rbida* questum / . . . *lege*sque u*rbe*sque ubi*cum*que (vv. 10–11); rhyming subjects: c*ohorte*s, *lege*s, *urbe*s, the first two anticipated by their parallel relative clauses in *quae*, the third rising to the crescendo of its 'Golden Line' variant, . . . *tua longin*quis | *implorant iura que*re*lis* / (vv. 9–12).[108] This babel of voices (re)produces the shout of happiness that Gallicus' poem exhorts itself to produce, up and down the hills of Rome; both will reproduce the cosmos of voices which has always, the poem shouts, turned its prayers in Gallicus' direction!

The priest-poet needs all Rome to echo his prayer for their old saviour, to make the prayer theirs and make it work. Bless the saviour who blesses their prayers to him with his ministrations. So let the throng join together to raise the roof in a triplet of joy. Let them bring their alacrity, rumpus and din, for an outburst of rapid-fire verbal pyrotechnics.[109] Again, all must answer the call because they are needed to drown out all other noises, which could only spoil this prayer on behalf of the community. One concerted whoop from Rome's Seven 'Hills', and there you have the *locus* of Roman identity, what makes 'us' us, an 'us', the (Flavian) 'us' of here and now.[110] Solidarity echoes, from Palatine to Capitoline, beating the bounds of social bonding through the Eternal City.

Statius' work, though, is not yet done. This last sentence has traded some more on the declarative force immanent in the present indicative tense. As if the habitual appeals of all and sundry are contemporaneous with the moment of the poem. But nothing masks the trajectory away into the chances of the subjunctive, however deafeningly the multitudes may wish away their lability. No sooner has Statius got the bells pealing and the hills alive with the sound of his music, than he stoops to repressing subversive dissent: his climax thrusts citizen tongues of malice under our noses where we cannot miss them. So not *all* Rome joins in the 'Halleluyahs', then. How else can Statius *police* Rome? Law enforcement officers need riot-squads, they need trouble-makers, and they need trouble (vv. 9–12). So, in their way, do prelates.

7

Saecular Fun and Games:
vv. 15–18

quippe manet longumque aeuo redeunte manebit
quem penes intrepidae mitis custodia Romae,   15
nec tantum induerint fatis noua saecula crimen
aut instaurati peccauerit ara Tarenti.

Still alive! Long as the aeon comes round again, he will live on—
in his hands, mild safe-guarding of an unruffled Rome—   15
and may the new age put so grave a charge upon fate,
nor let the altar of renewed Tarentum commit sin!

In this next burst, the proem gets back to Gallicus' bedside and desk,
bungs that little word '*Rome*' onto the scales, and ties the Prefect's
survival into the religious traditions that forge eternity. 'Gallicus looks
upon the stars' again (vv. 3f.): 'Still alive!'. In his one word, *manet*,
Statius throws in the full indicative weight of the present tense to assert,
in the teeth of the unmentionable bad news whose mention he just did
his worst to drown with noise and now sets himself to drown with more
affirmation. Make no mistake: this short dissyllable is the entire project.

Manet thrusts its truth-claim forward into the future: 'Gallicus
lives—and that's permanent'. Such an asseveration, we know ('Elvis
lives', 'Janis lives', 'Jimi lives', . . .), displays *will*, despite grammar.
Performatively, in talk, 'X lives!' *stresses* by denial mortal subjection
to 'Deathstiny' (*fatum*=death/fate) and *betrays* resistance to the
ineluctable. At once the point is yielded, as *manet* is supplemented
(completed and undone) by *manebit*. 'Gallicus *will* live on', then. In
manet . . . -que . . . manebit, Statius turns to the ritual formula of a
binding spell. Repetition will make the short sweet moment of
existence, *manet*, stretch into the long expanse of a future perdurance

beyond limit, *longumque aeuo redeunte manebit l.* Yes, Gallicus' recovery is now, and ever will be, bound into the pieties of patriotic ritual. In the process, the public servant is conflated with his city: 'Rome' is 'in his hands' (v. 16).

The survival of the Urban Prefect who has Rome in his safe-keeping must not be separable from the Eternal City he guards. Such is the compelling logic of Myth: Rome's calm custodian wards and calms the city; but the city could never fret; so by reflex the city protects its all-too-obviously vulnerable warder. Magic! Here's how it works: calming Myth cures fretting Romans; the power of Myth shields the guard with city ideology; the flow of symbolic power is reversed; civic discourse makes the state thrive, cohesive concord proves the health of the nation, and so Gallicus' problem prompts resolution, occasioning a new lease of life for the community.

Spot the anxieties held in negation, in *in-trepidae.* And see how the ellipsis of the verb (<'is'>) finesses choice of tense, taking the Urban Prefect (whose position, and this made it very likely that the job was a killer, could indeed go on and on, unlike those magistracies that went back to the Republic, unto the grave[111]) right out of human temporality. Statius is making Gallicus sound like Rome, like a consul, like a *soter* ('Saviour'), like an emperor, like a metonym for the Empire, like something important and permanent.

[1] *manet . . . manebit* belongs to the mantic language of patriotic prayer, along with 'He shall never change' and 'He shall stand firm, shall endure'.[112]

[2] *aeuo redeunte* inflects sacral/saecular formula, echoing the Sibylline/saecular Virg. *Ecl.* 4. 6, 'The Virgin returns and the reign of Saturn returns'.[113]

[3] *mitis*, a keyword in the pacific atmospherics of *Siluae*,[114] is also part of saecular discourse, as in 'mild Apollo' (Hor. *Carm. Saec.* 33, Tib. 2. 5. 79).[115]

Gallicus' affliction is blown up into a national ague, the health of Rome is condensed into the recovery of the Prefect. The emperor can now mediate between divine eternity and mortal ephemerality in preserving his/the state's intermediary. Rome was forever wishing its ruler *salus*,[116] and in praying that he save-and-be-saved, made him into *Salus* (e.g. 'Safe Rome—safe Fatherland—safe is Germanicus', Suet. *Gai.* 6). But the emperor's participation in the divine reprieve for mortality will prove so far from a sure stairway to transcendence that it rather deconstructs the imaging of imperial godhead as the irresistible power of divine medication. Domitian runs the same risk as any holy Healer, of being detachable from the divinity vested in his medicine, and so liable himself to be infected with its toxicity. Mythologic would say that in so far as Domitian is *not* like Gallicus, he *is* like Aesculapius; but in so far as he is like Aesculapius, he *is* like Gallicus. And if it doesn't already, this will, I promise, make sense before this book is done.

With his talk of the 'New Age' and 'the altar of Tarentum', Statius keys Gallicus' affliction still more directly into the health of the nation. Everyone 'knew' the *saecular games* had their origin in plague and pestilence,[117] whether or not they had taken their one chance to join in saecular prayers for 'the eternal salvation, victory, health of the Roman People'.[118] This once-in-a-lifetime festival *did* connote socio-political, national, moral, religious . . . crisis.[119] Critical illness in the Prefect of the City could well re-activate the very sort of alarm to which the saecular games tradition was pledged: conceivably (the details are lacking for 88), Gallicus played a part in the celebrations not unlike Agrippa's in 17 BCE, at the Princeps' right hand and helping to lead the several prayers.[120] In any case, Statius now represents Gallicus' illness as a vital, or mortal, threat to saecular propitiation, and so to national health, and imperial salvation.

Once more as we acclaim Gallicus' revival, we find our text wavers away from the constative confidence immanent in assertions made in the present and future indicative tenses: *manet* through *manebit* (and [ellipsis], vv. 15f.). This climax to our first prayerful hunk of poem wants to culminate in confirmatory congratulations. But once more unpropitious mentions of evil interrupt the felicitations. No, terrible crime or awful sin did *not* sour and darken the sweetness and light of Domitian's *saeculum*; heaven forbid, but why trouble to pray it would not? The words of the prayer surely cost more than they can earn, as the prominence of the 'hinge' term 'charge' insists (v. 17: *crimen* /). If euphemistic reticence plus technical phraseology can blot out their mention of ritual blighted, still any attempted realization of a future perfect indicative for *induerint . . . peccauerit* wavers in the utterance away to the precarious jussive perfect subjunctive *induerint . . . peccauerit*. Feel the trump of salvation decay into optative fragility.

Statius is trying to manoeuvre his Rome into assisting unbroken tradition to stay that way. Tradition-bound Rome secured its own sacredness by re-cycling its very own mumbo-jumbo—in 'instauration', of 'Tarentine' lore. Protected by the flexing of River Tiber, the strange liminal 'altar of Tarentum' keeps alive the aetiology of the saecular games, mapping the city from its furthest corner[121] and earthing the procession of rituals which wire all Rome through Palatine to Capitol (see Figure 5a). The original spooky tale bestows upon this purpose-made altar its peculiar and in perpetuity sacred name—as such, therefore, a *locus* for fervid disputation, starting with the spelling: *Tarenti* or *Terenti?*—and links it with the furthest end of Italy (heading south to Tarentum).[122] For his part, our Prefect comes to defend the Holy City from the northernmost boundary of Italy, where Turin was planted against the Gallic threat. This 'Guardian of the City' works, like altar ritual, to keep the 'inside' whole and extrude dissension, intervening against all 'crime' within his jurisdiction and set to prohibit all 'sin'.

The Urban Prefect has *imperium* vested in him to 'instaurate' proper order. Statius saw to it that Rome is properly turned-out for Gallicus. On parade, in court, and Sunday-best for church: 'Beefeater' cohorts tending their ensigns; uniformed lawyers distressed by mess; the civilized world designated by its robes (vv. 9–12); and, now, Roman Destiny must 'wear propitious blamelessness beyond cavil'.

> Let these prayers be spotlessly perfect—or they will spoil the rite.

> Let clean performance deliver efficacy, or rather, let's hope it will not rule out all chance of efficacy . . .

8

You Sing It, I'll Play It: vv. 19–37

ast ego nec Phoebum, quamquam mihi surda sine illo
plectra, nec Aonias decima cum Pallade diuas   20
aut mitem Tegeae Dircesue hortabor alumnum:
ipse ueni uiresque nouas animumque ministra
qui caneris; docto nec enim sine numine tantus
Ausoniae decora ampla togae centumque dedisti
iudicium mentemque uiris. licet enthea uatis   25
excludat Piplea sitim nec conscia detur
Pirene, largos potius mihi gurges in haustus
qui rapitur de fonte tuo, seu plana solutis
cum struis orsa modis seu cum tibi dulcis in artem
frangitur et nostras curat facundia leges.   30
quare age, si Cereri sua dona merumque Lyaeo
reddimus, et diues praedae tamen accipit omni
exuuias Diana tholo captiuaque tela
Bellipotens, nec tu (quando tibi, Gallice, maius
eloquium fandique opibus sublimis abundas)   35
sperne coli tenuiore lyra. uaga cingitur astris
luna et in oceanum riui cecidere minores.

Now, my Statius! No Apollo—though my picks are, without him,
deaf! No Béotiennes goddesses, into double figures, with Athena!   20
No mild fosterling of Tegea or Dirce, either, for my exhortation!
Come in person yourself, and serve new strength and spirit,

who art this song's subject! For, not without learnèd divine power
    your, greatness
conferred generous honours on the togas of old Italie, and on the
    Court
of One Hundred Men judicious intelligence! Inspired Piplea may shut   25
out bardic thirst and partnership may be denied
from Pirene: I prefer a flood for generous draughts
wolfed from the spring that you are—either when you build your
    level works
in measures free, or when sweet eloquence gets broken
into your artistry, and takes good care of our laws!   30
So on you go! If we grant Ceres her gifts and alcohol
is Bacchus', and for all her wealth in prey Diana still welcomes
    spoils
in her every rotunda, and captured arms are welcome
to the War-god, don't you—since you, Gallicus, own greater
eloquence, and with funds of speech overflow above
    elevation—   35
scorn worship from all too feather-weight a lyre! The roaming moon
    is encircled
by stars, and down into ocean pour rivulets of lesser volume.

The proem led us to the altar of 'Tarentum' and the Apollo-centred saecular processions from that holy spot. Now he has gathered and lathered his Roman choristers, the poet turns to call up a novel Apollo-figure for poetical/rhetorical inspiration: Gallicus himself! He offers a series of hymnal prayers to the divine inspiration of Gallicus, pouring the 'tiny rivulets' of verse Statius has to offer into an 'ocean' of reverence. So this will be a matching montage of prooemial material, not so much a start as a new preliminary. Calling on Gallicus elevates him above consideration of his demise, senescence and depletion. Now he is brimming with supernal vigour—a donor, curator, fund and charity. He is a power in the land, at law and at leisure. A god with Statius-minnows for acolytes: 'If not for you . . .'.[123]

This invocation re-writes into poetic/cultic (and second-person) terms Gallicus' performance of his duties as imperial servant. This time the dynamic duo are, not ruler and colleague, Domitian and Gallicus, but writer and hack, Gallicus and Statius, the assistant now the boss.[124] The best mouth to voice thanksgiving for Gallicus' rescue is the horse's. So, yes, apostrophe smuggles in a tribute of honorific praise (and, of course, re-asserts Gallicus' survival, with enhanced powers). But, I am bound to say for the last time, prayerful modality still applies. In this passage, constative content almost disappears: only 'you the subject of this song' (v. 23: *qui caneris*) uses a present indicative with *any* claim to include *any* declaration about the state of affairs obtaining at the moment—and *that* is a self-referential pointer to textual 'reality'! No. We must take the invocation trope at its word. These are *still* preliminaries to the promised work. We hover at the gate, *awaiting* poetic 'worship from all too feather-weight a lyre' (v. 36).[125] Where the proem drummed up voices to shout out joy, now the invocation begs Gallicus to put it into poetry. A life of public duty shaped the first overture; life-skills in the art(s) of blending Graeco-Roman culture animate the second.

Gallicus is fit for a poem from the poet laureate, because he is alive to Statius's intimacy with the Muses that helped write his grand Roman epic of Greek Thebes, and au fait with the allusive language spoken on Parnassus and on Palatine:

[1] '*Aonian* . . . goddesses with Athene' (v. 20) tells in up-market style of Cadmus' incorporation of the subjected local natives into his foundation of Thebes; 'Muses in Minerva's retinue' (v. 20) parades her patronage of artistic efflorescence under Domitian.[126]

[2] 'Nursling of Tegea or Dirce' (v. 21) veils in periphrasis the. *Thebaid*'s (anti-)hero Parthenopaeus and his birthplace in Arcadia, mother of pathos; and the Boeotian spring that marks doomed Thebes with sons' vengeance for mother Antiope's maltreatment.[127] Gallicus is ready to read *Statius*—he could've written *Thebaid*.

Together with the Hellenic mafia (*Phoebum . . . plectra . . ., Aonias . . . Pallade . . ., Tegeae Dircesue*, vv. 19–21), Gallicus' repertoire can set Roman authority—'the Ausonian toga' of Italy, and the centumuiral court of Rome' (vv. 23–5)[128]—in a Roman alliance of 'strength of mind', 'judgement and intelligence' (vv. 22, 25). So bands of females and bunches of boy-and-tom-boy-leaders in the imagination's play are spliced with the massed ranks of responsible Ro-Men, at their civic work. Gallicus lacks *numen* neither as inspired/inspirational poet nor as empowered Lawman, whose 'nod' enforces justice (v. 23). He matches Phoebus, we *docti* ('learnèd') realise, in twinning musework and supervision of the law.[129] The poem is a poem, but its prayers still make a plea—special pleading, that is, both for and from the bench!

In the next sentence (vv. 25–30), Statius shows off the civilizing synthesis of Greek fancy with Roman rules some more. First he plays the Neapolitan/cosmopolitan bilingual, toying with Greek words naturalized in Latin, a Roman game of Greek etymologies in a legal tussle:

[1] As Vollmer saw ((1971) 286 *ad loc.*), *Piplea* spells 'Saturating' (from **pimplêmi*) and *enthea* has 'god *inside*': so how *can* the poet's *thirst* be *shut out* from there (*excludat sitim*, vv. 25f.)? *Excludo* in a Roman court meant some, or any, form of 'debar' or 'prohibit'.

[2] *Pirene*, or 'Experienced' (from **peiraomai*), mock-translates as *conscia* (vv. 26f.). So 'she' *cannot* be '*neither admitted as accomplice before the fact nor produced in court as witness*' (*nec conscia detur /*: cf. *dedisti /*, v. 24, in court).

Next on the way through the sentence, Statius uses Latin to stir Graeco-Roman poetics into momentary conceit: Gallicus' creativity produces unCallimachean 'rapids in spate' from a Callimachean 'spring', a 'full draught' for tiny Statius of the *Siluae* (*largos . . . mihi gurges in haustus / qui rapitur de fonte tuo*, vv. 27f.).[130] And, finally, Statius compacts the Poesie and the Polizei in Gallicus' Roman lives in a striking impressionist take on aesthetics in his world of writing, presented in a vivacious vignette made this time from the most ordinary plainspeak:[131] good writing can be 'free-form' or 'law-abiding'; a 'free piece' is nevertheless 'built' and 'structured', a compromise between 'level' control and 'unleashed' release; 'a ready supply of words' needs to be 'broken into artwork' (vv. 28–30). Cross-over between the talent and technique it takes to write (poems such as) the *Siluae*, and the terms under which orators ply their trade before the Law, links like-minded wordsmiths to lawyers (*nostras . . . leges*, v. 30). True enough, they *were* regularly combined roles at, and in, court, and in his time Gallicus had been advocate and praetor before becoming Prefect.

And *now*: the build-up of the 'epiklesis' (appeal for epiphany) is done! We are ready to say why we're calling heaven (*quare age*, v. 31). Nearly ready. We *just* have to make sure we're not being pushy at the vital moment. We *only* have to be sure the prayer will be the right come-on for the right deity—take a moment, distending the sentence, for one or two final devotions. For Gallicus: perm Italian 'Ceres' with Grecian 'Bacchus' (*Lyaeus*); Diana's 'rotunda' (*tholo*) with Mars' 'arms' (*tela*);

the huntress' 'prey' and 'spoils' with the War-god's 'captured arms'; her 'wealth' with his 'power'. Set everything in place, say and show that is what you're doing.[132] This should guarantee a favourable reception—and pledges that this devotee knows his trade, and can deliver.

So we are there now: 'Don't you—' (v. 34). But no, it's not easy to ask gods not to do what is in their power to do, it only puts ideas into their heads! Statius interrupts himself just at the point where he gets to *the* point, and pops the question. He intrudes a polar pair of tributes, one starkly verbless and impersonally phrased for magniloquence in an instant, the other awash with luxuriant mixed metaphors (vv. 34–5). Can these last-gasp compliments assigning 'all power to the invoked deity alone' fit hymnal rhetoric to the poetics and politics of Statius' Gallicus?[133] So well that the defensive negativity may be blinked, recuperated, or relished? Let's see!

The prayer takes less than a line, when it comes: '[Don't you] scorn worship from all too feather-weight a lyre!' (v. 36). The 'learnèd godhead' (v. 23, *docto . . . numine*) of a Gallicus must know the trademark self-deprecation of Statius' comparatively 'fly-weight lyric' poetics for the Callimachean boast it flaunts. The gnome (proverb-like general reflection) that rounds off the invocation takes one step further the aggrandizement of Gallicus' status, by harping some more on the 'greatness' and 'abundance' which upturns Statius' Callimachean aesthetic values: when this cadence has 'minor tributaries' feed 'the ocean', the poet pictures himself as a 'small drop', but one among myriads that make their tiny contribution to singing 'as much as the sea'.[134] Just before that final phrase, Statius images Gallicus as another 'moon ringed with satellite stars', bringing the invocation full circle back to 'Apollo and his ten Muses', where we came in (vv. 19f.). So this 'Hymn to Gallicus' defined itself, all along, for those with ears to hear (vv. 19f.), as *another* 'Hymn to Apollo', one with a difference ('No Apollo! No Muses!'). In the same breath, Statius promised his new 'Hymn' would be *more on Thebes*, not more '*Thebaid*', but a lyric on Thebes' least gentle 'fosterling' (v. 21). Lovers of sublime Graeco-Latin lyric like Gallicus can't miss the carefully framed echo that frames his poem both generically and genealogically: Statius dares amplify *the* classic Olympian moment from *Horace's Pindaric lyre*. For Statius' closing verse: / luna *et in oceanum riui cecidere* minores / ('. . . / the moon, and into ocean fall minor streams /', v. 37) *parades* reference to the great religious-political Augustan Ode *Quem uirum aut heroa* (*Carm.* 1. 12. 46ff.):[135]

55

. . . micat inter omnes
Iulium sidus uelut inter ignis
/ luna minores. //

> . . . there flashes among them all
> the Julian star, like the *moon* among the
> *minor* points of light.

Horace's hymn continues from this Julian climax to its procession of honoured Roman heroes of the Republic, to pair the Almighty Jove with his adjutant Caesar: 'Father of the human race and its guardian, born of Saturn, in your care is put the destiny of mighty Caesar' (49–52).[136] So there is mileage in analogizing that Gallicus is, for the likes of Statius, an Apollo and Augustus rolled-into-one, vice-gerents with special responsibilities delegated to them by transcendent Father Jupiter. The Urban Prefect shadows *his* Augustus closely—Domitian the universal soldier, orator, poet (Sil. 3. 614–21):[137]

hic et ab Arctoo currus aget axe per urbem,
ducet et Eoos . . . triumphos.
idem . . . uictor compescet sedibus Histrum.
quin et Romuleos superabit uoce nepotes,
quis erit eloquio partum decus. huic sua Musae
sacra ferent, meliorque lyra, cui substitit Hebrus
et uenit Rhodope, Phoebo miranda loquetur.

Domitian shall both drive his chariot through Rome from the north
    pole's axle
and head triumphs . . . over Dawn's east.
Victorious, he shall confine Danube in its place.
Why, he will, too, outmatch for voice the grandsons of Romulus
who have won glory from eloquence. To him the Muses
shall bring their holy rites, and his lyre, better than the one which
    halted Hebrus
and drew Rhodope, will speak songs to make Phoebus marvel.

So now the invocation is made. We could say it amounts to a prooemial *captatio beneuolentiae*. All Statius wanted was for Gallicus not to turn his nose up at *Siluae* 1. 4. Not much to ask! And if this 'Hymn' has gone 'phut' in terms of getting anywhere, information-wise, with the here-and-now business afoot, it has at any rate prepared us for a Graeco-Roman, post-Callimachean/post-Horatian, lyric assault on Parnassus. And the idea running through all the posturing and play-acting is that a 'Hymn to Hymning' must win over its readers, and charm all Malice away.[138] 'Don't scoff' doesn't take long to say, but a short poem needs all the help it can get if it is not to fall on its face.

As the invocation 'falls away in diminuendo' (v. 37), the next chapter is ready and we are readied to start the poem where the poem starts up for real. Now we're in the right mood. (It *would* be Malice to take with us the thought that Statius has just as good as invited us, with Gallicus, to own up that he is a lousy subject for the *Siluae*, far too grand a busybody to hear it when he is told there is no music in Statius if Apollo and the rest of the gang are pushed out and the poet banned from his natural habitat, a heavyweight muscle-man and know-all who crashes the recital with a whirl of his own all-purpose rhetoric and, if he *is* to get what he is due, would be best off writing his own ode . . . In the (parathetic) insertion that divides the nub of Statius' prayer from its governing negative, 'Don't you ‖ . . . ‖ scorn' (vv. 34–6), a gap opens between poet and addressee that no equivocation and undifferentiation between them can ever finally close. The modern history of reading the *Siluae* has pretty well consisted of precisely the scorn that Statius invites from us Gallicuses. But that was *then*. Now the prayers are said! Let's kick Envy out of the book, to follow Malice!)

9

You Had Us All Worried There:
vv. 38–49

quae tibi sollicitus persoluit praemia morum
Vrbis amor! quae tum patrumque equitumque notaui
lumina et ignarae plebis lugere potentes!   40
non labente Numa timuit sic curia felix
Pompeio nec celsus eques nec femina Bruto.
hoc illud, tristes inuitum audire catenas,
parcere uerberibus nec qua iubet alta potestas
ire, sed armatas multum sibi demere uires   45
dignarique manus humiles et uerba precantum,
reddere iura foro nec proturbare curules
et ferrum mulcere toga. sic itur in alta
pectora, sic mixto reuerentia fidit amori.

What returns for your ethics were paid you in full by concerned
love from Rome¹/₂ What messages I made out back then, in the eyes
    of senators, equestrians,
and proletariat, which doesn't bother much with mourning
    rulers¹/₂   40
No, when Numa was slipping away the blessed Senate-house didn't
    dread this way,
nor the equestrians on high when it was Pompey, nor each woman
    when Brutus.
This was a case of: never liking to hear grim shackles,
easy on the beatings and no going along with commands from
    authority

above, but plenty of self-denial in using the armed forces,   45
and respect for humble prayers, gestured or spoken,
guaranteeing justice in court and no pushing the magistrates out of
   the way
and steel softened with civil dress. This is the way to the depth
of hearts, this way respect trusts blended love.

The body of the poem (vv. 38–114) is set firmly in the past! What does the present recounting of *The Life of Gallicus* amount to?[139] Exclamatory narration from the relieved poet who relives the nightmares of the story he recounts! An opportunity to ask what Rome really felt about its government, all that they had to thank the empire for, their way of life?

   There are several narratives to follow, before Statius is done. In this first one, we hear that Rome loves its Gallicus, why respect goes deep (vv. 39, 48f.).[140] As in the proem, gratitude for Gallicus' praefectorial work brings the city out to pray. Old Rome, *echt* Rome *Ab Urbe Condita* through the Republic, comes out in force, 'Senators and equestrians and—for all their engrained irreverence—plebs' (vv. 39f.). Gallicus joins a trio of beloved Roman *exempla* across the aeons, heroized alongside King Numa, Pompey the Great (with his rival, Sulla Felix, shadowed in *felix /*, v. 41), and Brutus (or rather, *both* Brutuses, first consul and founder of the Republic, *and* Julius Caesar's tyrannicide, at the other end of the verse from / *Pompeio*, v. 42). They intimate death, and figure anxieties for one at death's door, covering all the possible narratives in prospect:

[1] Numa, the last Roman King to die naturally, 'met no swift or sudden end', but at just over eighty 'little by little through old age and a gentle disease faded away'. His funeral was a national celebration of totally realized peace, senators carrying the bier, priests for escort, everyone there as if burying their nearest and dearest.[141] An enviable prospect, if death could count as such.

[2] Pompey *recovered* from his grave illness, in 50 BCE, and was fêted by the populations of Naples, where they 'gave thanksgiving sacrifice for his recovery', the rest of Campania, and all of Italia; but this only shot him full of false optimism and, the moral runs on, he would in hindsight have got lucky if he *had* died at this his zenith, before losing his head on the shores of Egypt. Pompey's affinity to the equestrian order bespoke the heroic/transgressive

triumphs he held 'before admission to the senate'; but, more pointedly, as founder of Rome's grandest theatre, he is acclaimed as the 'tallest' of Horace's 'tall *Ramnes*' (= *equites*).[142]

[3] *Et tu, Brute*. When the matrons mourned the first Brutus he was, like Numa, well and truly dead and communally lamented.[143] Add just a hint of defeated suicide, courtesy of Brutus the tyrannicide.

So Statius recaptures mortal fear for the latest in the long line of great Romans. How could Gallicus earn this status? This is where the poem faces its toughest test, set to praise the *praefectura urbis* within the *political* traditions of the Roman state. Bravura, inconcinnity, the huff-and-puff of hyperbole are inescapable. Statius insulates his account of sound administration by presenting it as a stereotype in précis (*hoc illud* . . ., v. 43). But if the incorrigible *plebs Romana* 'resist giving the nobs a proper send-off' (v. 40), they could be reminding us of good reasons *not* to bother to get to know the Chief of Security any better, dead or alive. If Romans 'weren't afraid *this way*' in the past (vv. 41f.), could that be because *their* heroes (and anti-heroes) really *had* won their affections? The iron fist shows through the velvet glove, as it must: always *hating* having to lock people up; sparing the rod; declining to follow orders no matter where; self-denial of strong-arm tactics to a considerable extent; respect for humble petitions and appeals; delivering justice in court without treading all over the magistrates; giving guns a soft-focus civilian feel (vv. 43–8). It could have been worse—but how glamorous can maintaining public order, punishing petty crime, hearing accusations from slaves, patrons and mugged, ever get?[144] The place booked in the hearts of throwback Roman nostalgia comes down to this: though he commanded a garrison, those (three) urban cohorts (v. 9),[145] the Urban Prefect *dressed as a senator* (Statius' last word, v. 48: *toga*). Quirky hints of Virgil fix the text up some,[146] until citation surfaces, ambitiously, linking into the reprise:

[1] Gallicus' daily dose of mildness 'softens steel and wins hearts' (vv. 48f., mulce*re* . . ., pectora)—like Virgil's Great Man In A Tight Simile, salving a riot by 'softening hearts' (*Aen*. 1. 153, pectora mulce*t*). Such 'softening' is what *Siluae* do best.[147] In 1. 4, Gallicus personifies the benign clemency that his poem enacts in the space filled by the prayers of Rome to soften the adamantine necessity of mortality.

[2] These same 'hearts' re-write, in *displayed* citation, Virgilian Apollo's praise for *his* favourite Julian protégé: 'A blessing on your tiro courage, child, this is the way to the stars, born of gods and someday father of gods' (*Aen.* 9. 641f., . . . sic itur *ad* astra, /) is deepened by Statius to: 'This is the way to the depth of hearts' (vv. 48f., sic itur *in* alta / *pectora* . . .). As often, Latin textuality plays between *altus* as 'high/deep' (e.g. vv. 44, 48): Statius' lyric means to internalize and emotionalize the external cosmos of power and the universe where Virgil's heroes live. Infinities of the heart.

So keep off others' patches, and don't come the old soldier—that's the ticket!

A nice try, but as Statius closed the circle in the middle of his list of Things you could like about Roman life under Gallicus, by recalling that 'prayers' heard with leniency generated a city's worth of prayers for a reprieve for Gallicus, to stay in the land of the living, nevertheless he made the city's anxieties already look ahead to the time when Gallicus must be dead, too—*just because of* that look back over (all) his dead predecessors and precedents. In the details of Gallicus' malaise, we are about to find a similar irony. The *soteria* implies *consolation* for the death it wants to proclaim defeated.

> And all these exclamations have to be read, as well, as questions!

> All these exclamations have to be read, as well, as questions?

10

At Death's Door:
vv. 50–7

ipsa etiam cunctos grauis inclementia fati   50
terruit et subiti praeceps iuuenile pericli
nil cunctante malo. non illud culpa senectae
(quippe ea bis senis uixdum orsa excedere lustris)
sed labor intendens animique in membra uigentis
imperium uigilesque suo pro Caesare curae,   55
dulce opus—hinc fessos penitus subrepsit in artus
insidiosa quies et pigra obliuio uitae.

In fact it was the unmerciful tyranny of Deathstiny united them   50
in terror, and the headlong vigour of the instant crisis
as the pox never paused. That was no fault of ageing
(indeed that had only just set to leaving three score years behind)
but the strain of hard work, and an energetic mind's command
over body parts, and unresting care upon care in serving your
    Caesar,   55
the job its own satisfaction . . .—And so there sneaked deep into
    exhausted limbs
the siege of leave, and comatose forgetting to live.

Alarm was exacerbated by the nature of the illness—its gravity, and a
strange combination of suddenness and stealth. 'Terror' triggers our
most detailed account of the affliction, another unforgiving ordeal for

the poet to survive, the prognosis might read, let alone turn into his finest hour. The ailment is terrifyingly instant, non-stop, in as good nick as our mature Prefect himself. Worry is mimed by syntactical breakdown, on the way toward registering the psychophysical collapse:

[1] The oppressive verbal weight of Fate (v. 50) starts terror at the turn of the verse, which becomes the hinge of the sentence, as the sudden, headlong rush of adjectival forms seems to presage danger still awaiting clarification; without the slightest hesitation, the run of words lapses into a fade-out of evil, . . . *malo* . . ., brought to an abrupt halt by *non* . . . (v. 52). Now we find this spill of words has made a supplementary subject for *terruit* and that no noun is pending for *iuuenile*, which must instead *calque* (stand in cross-lingually for) the Greek 'definite article+neuter of the adjective' idiom for (what *we* have to label) an abstract concept: 'the quality of youthfulness=impetuosity=*to neanikon=praeceps*'.

[2] The 'no' introduces negative description, prompted by the sugges-tion in *iuuenile* that frailty is part of the pattern of mortality: 'No, *not* a case of *young* disease rampant over *ageing* human' (v. 52).

[3] A momentary parenthesis annotates the point. In a different tone, not really part of the poem at all, a self-contained verse to read and at once discount, the nugatory aside enacts what it says, for *its weaving* does not *exceed* its *hexa*meter unit of measurement, by doubling into a second verse, not at all, not even a tiny bit (v. 53: *bis* senis *uixdum* orsa excedere *lustris*).[148]

[4] Neither interjected denial nor its 'footnote' took the time and trouble to afford their verbs 'to be', but the 'but . . .' clause we could anticipate as re-phrasing the denial in positive form extends into a staccato catalogue of factors 'A+B+C' (vv. 54f.) before the minimal supplement of an apposition is interrupted and, ensuring no main verb can materialize, we collapse into anacolouthon: . . .— *hinc* . . . (v. 56).

Not only is it hard to talk terror straight, but a poetic Gallicus must deserve special illness so that he can deserve special treatment. The switchback sentence grapples with the task of setting up a miracle cure for a fascinating patient ('Why are other people's crack-ups so boring?'), and fight off the mundanity of sexagenarian trauma ('After all, things *do* start to wear out . . .').

At his peak, this veteran guardsman, a trooper through and through, was infiltrated by a stealthy third-column, in a chronic siege of the body's defensive positions, or immunity systems. Kept taut and fit by work, in proper and efficient command of himself, no hostile elements could catch him napping; never off-guard in defence of the realm, he made his job his life. Just doing it gave him all he wanted. But he did give it his all, and the moment he took a break and went off-duty, his own defences were down, and in stormed narcosis, patiently waiting on the chance to clinch the siege—the fate awaiting all armies of occupation running down through shortage of action.[149] Gallicus' blindspot was, of course, that he *had* got 'lazy', in just one respect: he had 'forgotten' how to look after Number One.[150] Such a poetic affliction: wasted by selflessness. Classic(al) workaholism, as clear a case as a Good Company or College or Department Man(ager) could ever want to imagine. Beautifully couched as dutiful neglect, this disease describes the syndrome of *power*.

But Statius will triangulate Gallicus' work, his illness and its cure, with the mytho-logical conclusion that the *real* sickness was the community's worry over its servant. Rome thought just-turned-sixty Gallicus would die of mortality in general, and this was his own special brand; but his lead shows how the health of Rome can be preserved (cured, cared for, saved . . .). In caring so much for their favourite minister, because *he* cared so much, the city can move mountains—roll back the weave of Deathstiny. Or at least give their very own 'Palinurus' a decent send-off?[151]

If *this* is the vision that Gallicus' breakdown occasions, was(n't) embarrassment with the need to provide humdrum 'facts' about it worthwhile? Thanksgiving may be an option in the repertoire of panegyric, but it does oblige you to show *some* concern for the relevant plight: no one's to shrug at time-expired Gallicus' weekend in hell. Mortal sickness prompted loving concern among friends, Romans, fellow-humans. Together with their urgent prayers of intercession, the paradoxical diagnosis, 'forgetfulness *of life*' reverberates loud enough to recall the god who has cared precious little for his protégé, the poet-at-law: . . . *obliuio uitae. / tunc deus . . .. securus* (vv. 57–60). Just as civic proem gave way to divine invocation, so civic panic leads to divine intervention.[152] Faith is displaced upwards in the mythic narration, which is enshrined at the heart of the concentric poem of praise (vv. 58–114). When we emerge from the miracle cure, we descend to find Statius fretting outside Gallicus' door, hoping everyone's prayers will be answered (vv. 115–22). He has gathered together Rome, the gods, and the poet, at Gallicus' sick-bed, ready to rejoin the moment of salvation for renewed acclamation (vv. 123–31). With that, the ring is closed, and in no time at all, just the minutes it takes to shout 'Hosanna!' and promise to pay what was vowed, we have saved (a) *Life at Rome.*

This is the place to present *Siluae* 1. 4 in panorama, since the awakening, epiphany, entry, and doctoring of Apollo & son (have) stop(ped) the human clock. No time passes in Rome while the gods operate. At the time, the suspense was killing; but now the narration takes none of our time. Time can never go slow enough when you're in heaven: the best way to spin it out is to dwell happily on how painfully time dragged before happiness arrived, how long it hurt when you were excruciated by terror. So let's overflow spontaneously with emotion recollected in tranquillity: a translation of the whole poem will take up the next chapter.

It will be over in a flash, and then everyone can start feeling better already (about Statius, for a start, who has been the answer to all our prayers from the very beginning). It wasn't that all those preliminaries kept us waiting for 'the action', just as it won't be keeping *us* waiting at Gallicus' threshold while we hear the story of 'the action' told, since we have been whooping up Graeco-Roman paeans in Statius' City choir from the start. It may've just felt that way before we were shown the light, found out what the thanksgiving was for, and, uplifted, entered lyric time(lessness).

11

Translation of Statius, *Siluae* 1. 4

You are there, yea, gods above, and this side of inexorability Fate
  Clotho
whirls her spinning work! Motherly Astraea looks upon the
  godfearing, and reconciled
with Jove she returns, and there gazes, too, upon the stars feared
  lost
Gallicus! You have heaven's heart, Germanicus, you have the gods'!
Who would deny it? Too embarrassed to strip the great servant
  from   5
your empire—that's Lady Luck! Stands right by your side, head
  unbowed
by the infinite burden, and old age's threads laden with loss
he sloughs, and finds himself growing young again, his better years
  up ahead!
Wherefore, platoons that look lively, tending the ensigns of Rome;
law after law that takes sanctuary in your arms, protesting   10
breaches of the peace, and the Roman towns wherever
that appeal for your arbitration in telegrammed disputes:
let them all compete in happiness, let our every hill in due sequence
roar in concert! And let mutterings from no-good gossip hold their
  peace!
Still alive! Long as the aeon comes round again, he will live on—   15

in his hands, mild safe-guarding of an unruffled Rome—
and may the new age put so grave a charge upon fate,
nor let the altar of renewed Tarentum commit sin!

Now, my Statius! No Apollo—though my picks are, without him,
deaf! No Béotiennes goddesses, into double figures, with Athena!   20
No mild fosterling of Tegea or Dirce, either, for my exhortation!
Come in person yourself, and serve new strength and spirit,
who art this song's subject! For, not without learnèd divine power,
    your greatness
conferred generous honours on the togas of old Italie, and on the
    Court
of One Hundred Men judicious intelligence! Inspired Piplea may
    shut   25
out bardic thirst and partnership may be denied
from Pirene: I prefer a flood for generous draughts
wolfed from the spring that you are—either when you build your
    level works
in measures free, or when sweet eloquence gets broken
into your artistry, and takes good care of our laws!   30
So on you go! If we grant Ceres her gifts and alcohol
is Bacchus', and for all her wealth in prey Diana still welcomes
    spoils
in her every rotunda, and captured arms are welcome
to the War-god, don't you—since you, Gallicus, own greater
eloquence, and with funds of speech overflow above elevation—   35
scorn worship from all too feather-weight a lyre! The roaming
    moon is encircled
by stars, and down into ocean fall rivulets of lesser volume.

What returns for your ethics were paid you in full by concerned
love from Rome¹/? What messages I made out back then, in the eyes
    of senators, equestrians,
and proletariat, which doesn't bother much with mourning rulers¹/?   40
No, when Numa was slipping away the blessed Senate-house didn't
    dread this way,
nor the equestrians on high when it was Pompey, nor each woman
    when Brutus.
This was a case of: never liking to hear grim shackles,
easy on the beatings and no going along with commands from
    authority

above, but plenty of self-denial in using the armed forces,   45
and respect for humble prayers, gestured or spoken,
guaranteeing justice in court and no pushing the magistrates out of
    the way
and steel softened with civil dress. This is the way to the depth
of hearts, this way respect trusts blended love.

In fact it was the unmerciful tyranny of Deathstiny united them   50
in terror, and the headlong vigour of the instant crisis
as the pox never paused. That was no fault of ageing
(indeed that had only just set to leaving three score years behind)
but the strain of hard work, and an energetic mind's command
over body parts, and unresting care upon care in serving your
    Caesar,   55
the job its own satisfaction . . .—And so there sneaked deep into
    exhausted limbs
the siege of leave, and comatose forgetting to live.

Then the god who by the heights on Alpine shoulders
seals the groves 'Apollo's' with his holy name,
takes a look, alas!, so great a fosterling and so long since he cared,   60
and cutting out obstacles, 'Away with me, my child from
    Epidaurus,
away', he said, 'come and be glad: it falls to us (must grab the
    opening)
to resurrect a massive hero. Let's set to, hold fast
the spindles eking out the end of the thread. No need to fear that
    black-out
thunderbolt, Jupiter will come out in favour, approve this use of our
    art.   65
Because it is no prole or godlessly unblessed
soul I save. And just as briefly as this, while we come up to his
    home,
I shall clarify all. His family's one-man pedigree, his aristocracy is
a posteriori, and his origin isn't lost, but by the light that's come
    after
is overcome and is glad of a mighty grandson to defer to.   70
He too won civil excellence, first in line, as bright and massive
in oratory. At once, in ops. at bases beyond count,
in stations of sunset and early dawn, under every sun there is,
the hand that took the oath saw service through, and peacetime
    stand-down, use of,

68

permission denied, no let-up of adrenalin or gunbelt unbuckled. 75
Galatia at its acme found nerve to go for him on their war-path
(me, too!) and nine harvests on end he scared Pamphylia
and Pannonian wildness, and fearful for artillery in tactical retreat
Armenia, and the River Araxes, finally putting up with a Roman
    bridge.
Why need I unfurl twin *fasces* and iterate jurisdiction over 80
mighty Asia? Indeed Asia would willingly have herself three goes
    and more
at him, but homeward calls the Official Calendar, and more than
    one promise
of a bigger desk. Take the miracle of tribute taxed from Libya,
in full cooperation, a triumph crated back from a hot-bed of
    peace—what point
in praise from me, vast riches not even the job creator was nerved 85
to anticipate? Gladness for Trasimene and Alps
and souls at Cannae, and first up for a badge-of-honour tribute,
there was Regulus, in no uncertain terms, a ghostly ball of
    happiness large as life.
No room for armies from the far north and the Rhine back to war
and captive Veleda's curses and—this the latest and mother 90
of all sagas—Rome in his safe-keeping during the Dacian massacre,
epics to open wide, that time the call came to take so great a
    driver's reins,
Gallicus, without a flicker of surprise from Fortune, and you took
    them up.

This one, then, if what I say is no disgrace, we'll snatch from the
    foul play
of Jupiter, son. This request is from the famed father of the City 95
and he has it owing. For it was not in vain that you boys recently
uttered my songs of praise in your patrician purple.
Anything in twin Chiron's health-bearing cave,
any herb; whatever Troy's Pergamum stores in your
rotunda; or Epidaurus' blessed spa on the beach 100
educates in her nursery; the one Crete has carpet the shade of Ida,
bloom of dittany's potency; and the snake's spate of
spit . . .—I can apply dexterity, plus every kindly
poison that in Arabia's scent-prolific fields the learnèd
shepherd gathered me, or else from the sward of Amphrysus'. 105

His speech was done. They find his limbs by now slackly sprawled
and his soul making a stand. Both gird themselves in the ceremonial
    style
of Paeon and together they gesture and they obey with a will,
until death-laden plague, versus manifold medication,
and coma's glowering cloudbanks of sick sleep were shattered by
    them.   110
The patient helps the gods and more than a match for any affliction
he gets in before help comes. No swifter a revival by
Haemonian skill was Telephus', nor panicked Menelaus'
raw wounds knitting through Machaon's elixir.

What space among all these gatherings of the Roman people and
    Fathers,   115
could there be for my prayerful care? Yet I call to witness the
    towering
stars and you, from Thymbra, father of bards, what all through
the daylight, all night, was the fear I felt, while clinging to the
    doorway
in twenty-four hour surveillance, varying ear with eye, I staked out
the lot, just as when, on tow from an aircraft-carrier,   120
a tiny dinghy, once the storm rages, takes its proportion of raving
waters, scaled down, and rolls under the same sou'wester.

Twine the thread to a sheen! Be glad now, sisters,
Twine on, let none reckon the limit of time passed!
Today will be the birth-day of his life. You are worth it: Trojan   125
aeons and the years' heap of Euboean dust, Sibyl,
and of mouldered Nestor. With what incense-bowl should my
    humble self now
gain you the propitiation you are worth? No, not if Mevania should
    empty her dales,
or Clitumnus' fresh-tilled fields afford snow-white bulls,
should I be enough. Though the gods have often, in the company of
    these offerings,   130
been won by turf and barley-meal, with just a shake of the salt-
    cellar.

Note: I have followed the text of Courtney (1990), but removed *lacunae*
after vv. 6, 61a, 73 and *obeli* at vv. 13, 45, suppressed v. 86a, and
accepted Housman's *praecidens* at v. 61. I accept the more salty *benigne*

at v. 103, but contrive to translate as if *benignum*: I found the *word* 'kindly' just too much of a treat, a rare adjective / adverb homophone.

This note is a reminder, in the absence of any *apparatus criticus* such as any scholarly edition of a classical text must always present, that we are able to read what we can of *Roman Life on paper* because of a stupendous investment of applied energy through two millennia of European, and more recently global, history. The survival of the *Siluae* in their one manuscript, found near L. Constance by Poggio in 1417/18, whose copy G. Loewe found in the National Library of Madrid in 1879, is as brute a testimony to the cultural hegemony of classical texts as it was a bizarre story of contingency, inadvertence, and chance (Figure 6). But for the monks of St Gallen, from these five books of poetry known at least fitfully through the centuries of reading in the Roman Empire, if scarcely beyond it, we would have just *Siluae* 2. 7, excerpted and preserved separately because it commemorates the

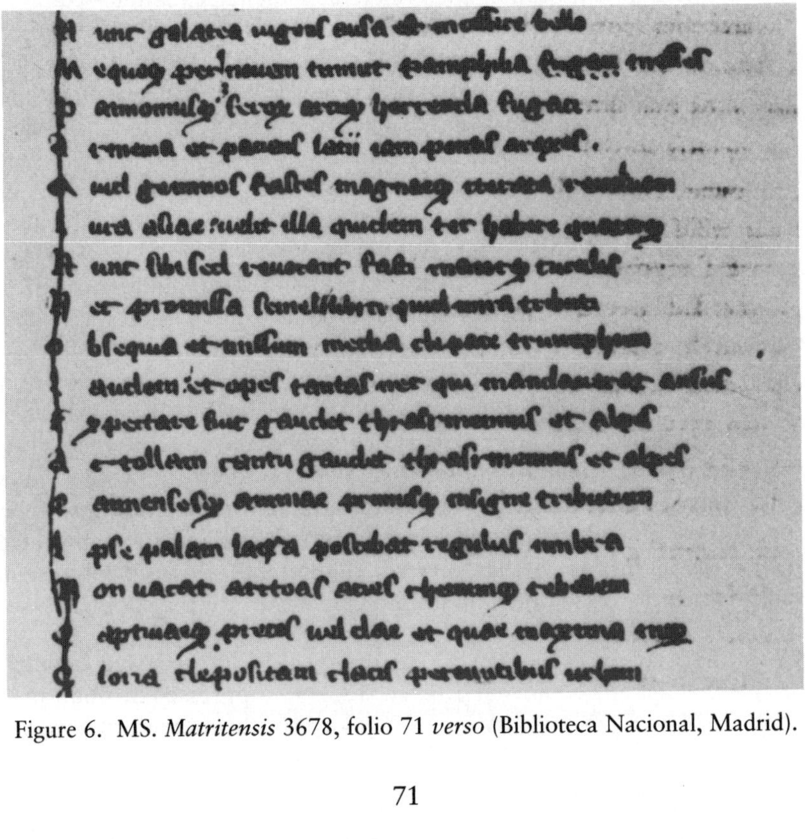

Figure 6. MS. *Matritensis* 3678, folio 71 *verso* (Biblioteca Nacional, Madrid).

birthday of Lucan, the explosive Latin epic poet of Roman civil war. This poem gives a strong reading of Lucan's *Roman Life*, appropriating his poetic and his martyrdom (executed for joining a conspiracy to assassinate Nero) as the most vital precursor for Statius' own traumatic epic of *mythic* civil war, the *Thebaid*.[153] But its claim to be the fittest of the *Siluae* for survival is that it attaches itself to a classic host (who also anticipated Statius in writing (lost) *Siluae*).

As it happens, the Madrid manuscript needs rescuing from its scribe, itself and its ancestors, if it is to get us close to reading what Statius thought he had written:

> *hoc opus, uno codice saeculi quinti decimi eoque ab homine ignarissimo omnium uiuentium scripto traditum, passim penitusque corruptum ad nos peruenit.*[154]

The lively interest taken by Italian humanists in their re-discovery of the *Siluae* can be documented in detail; and a long roll-call of works devoted to their explication and (where possible) emendation—editions, commentaries, articles, and books—represents a vast collective project within the reading-cultures developed in the print society of the world so far. The story is briskly told by Courtney (1990) *Praefatio*—told (as I expect you noticed) *in Latin*, to keep the flag flying over classical scholarship, with its internationalist traditions and convictions . . .[155]

It is not surprising either that this book had plenty of choice for an image of Domitian (Figure 3) or that it had none at all for Rutilius Gallicus, lost once his statue and its base went their separate ways, somewhere along the road between Flavian and Byzantine Ephesos. If it is odd not to have an ancient *Statius* to point to, that is on the mighty *Thebaid*'s account. As we shall see in chapter 19, the author of *Siluae* knew from the start that his best bet for eternity, in two or three dimensions, was always going to be to cling to his own epic coat tails! Nevertheless, the 'off-camera' shots of courtier culture somewhere close to the zenith of imperial *Life at Rome* that *Siluae* provide helped élites in Europe to fit reading and literature, arts and humanities, into their conception of civilized existence in as direct and seemingly unmediated a fashion as any texts that survive (chapter 20). Today's interest in cultural history kicks these Nestorian ephemera into the spotlight once more.

12

He's in Gods' Hands Now:
vv. 58–62, 106

tunc deus, Alpini qui iuxta culmina dorsi
signat Apollineos sancto cognomine lucos,
respicit heu tanti pridem securus alumni.   60
praecidensque moras:

. . . ait . . .
   . . .
dixerat.   106

Then the god who by the heights on Alpine shoulders
seals the groves 'Apollo's' with his holy name,
takes a look, alas!, so great a fosterling and so long since he cared,   60
and cutting out obstacles, . . .

. . . he said . . .
   . . .
. . . His speech was done.   106

Invocation of Apollo delivered Romans a powerful tradition of inclusive culture-myths and cult-practices, communal sources of the sense of belonging. However they might put this to themselves or to each other, the same flow of symbolic knowledge-and-power ran through the courtiers who 'just' stage-managed the ceremonies of the saecular games, and now read pretty obeisance to Gallicus in Statian conceit. As we shall see (chapter 15, *Appendix*), if Apollo brings 'joy' to Gallicus'

City of terror (vv. 62, 70, 86, 88), with his son Aesculapius he also brings heroic trauma to the role of the emperor's lieutenant. Statius' myth finds leverage in Graeco-Roman myth for thinking Flavian government. Autocracy is created and maintained by such performatives; theocracy provides a register where power can also be disassembled, explored, and even deprecated.[156]

As the poem cumulates behind its prayer a universe strung from petitions, petitioners, appeals and repetitions, the poet-priest pledges Rome to renew commitment to the entire politico-religious apparatus. Apollo comes to acknowledge the hierarchies and institutions that were realized in performance of the rites of the *ludi saeculares* of 88 for the gods, for Apollo and for Father Jupiter, under the *Pontifex Maximus* Domitian, under the *Praefectus Urbi* Gallicus. Those rites were vocalized in the singing of the 'freshly composed' *carmen saeculare*, represented here by Statius (vv. 95–7).[157]

But, far from allowing 'the logic of the *soteria*' to *guarantee* anything, by 'rhetorical prescription', Apollo's myth articulates the precarious complexity of temporality in thanksgiving. The poem proposes, rather than presupposes, a cure. It 'implies that the illness and cure' are 'narrated . . . as past occurrences', but *cannot* state or declare that the cure is secure, perfect, preterite, over and done with.[158] In fact, Syme put it in a nutshell: Statius 'offers up vows that Rutilius Gallicus be restored to health'.[159] Apollo will come as close as he dares to underwriting our acclamation of Gallicus' restoration; but his epiphany actually serves to explore the necessary transcendence of cosmic (in)exorability at an echelon higher up in the scheme of things. The prayer that rejoices that prayers may be heard wants to prove that a prayer has been heard; but there must always be reservations made. Even a god who hears prayers, and decides to answer them, must work within the axiom that this is subject to denial, revision, cancellation. The *soteria* is an occasion not to forget that what destiny gives humans is subject to the ephemeral temporality of mortality: it must be provisional, conditional, precarious. If acclamation takes *any* of this time, it risks hybristic self-confutation!

Apollo will exude his usual balm, and ooze charm:[160] but he is *also* Statius' opportunity to warn us that we are meant to die, and die we must. The limitations on saecular renewal of the Eternal City of Rome just edge into view. Not even the emperor, or the son of the Almighty, can hand Rome forever on a plate: they must just keep right on praying, and take what comes.[161]

13

The VIP Treatment:
vv. 61–8, 94–7

... *'hinc mecum, Epidauria proles,*
hinc' ait 'i gaudens: datur (aggredienda facultas)
ingentem recreare uirum. teneamus adorti
tendentes iam fila colos. ne fulminis atri
sit metus: has ultro laudabit Iuppiter artes,   65
nam neque plebeiam aut dextro sine numine cretam
seruo animam. atque adeo breuiter, dum tecta subimus,
expediam ...

hunc igitur, si digna loquor, rapiemus iniquo,
nate, Ioui. rogat hoc Latiae pater inclitus Vrbis   95
et meruit; neque enim frustra mihi nuper honora
carmina patricio, pueri, sonuistis in ostro.'

... 'Away with me, my child from Epidaurus,
away', he said, 'come and be glad: it falls to us (must grab the
      opening)
to resurrect a massive hero. Let's set to, hold fast
the spindles eking out the end of the thread. No need to fear that
      black-out
thunderbolt, Jupiter will come out in favour, approve this use of our
      art.   65
Because it is no prole or godlessly unblessed

75

soul I save. And just as briefly as this, while we come up to his home,
I shall clarify all . . .

. . . This one, then, if what I say is no disgrace, we'll snatch from the foul play
of Jupiter, son. This request is from the famed father of the City   95
and he has it owing. For it was not in vain that you boys recently
uttered my songs of praise in your patrician purple.'

Apollo asks/tells his son to join him, and stop destiny in its tracks. So they (will) do: with the patient's help (vv. 106–14). Apollo tells us he 'brings salvation', here, now (v. 67). 'He and his son' (*uterque*, v. 107), must be the 'gods' of the miracle cure (v. 111). Apollo dispels fear, of a bolt from Father Jove, for undoing inexorable Deathstiny. Why take the risk and put himself outside Olympian law, just for a World Power's worth of loving prayers? Because the patient 'deserves' salvation, both in his right, for 'serving' Rome (v. 74, *permeruit*, cf. *praemia*, v. 38), and because his Lord (Domitian) 'deserves' repayment for celebrating Apollo in the songs freshly sung at his (their) saecular games (v. 96, *meruit*). And 'dignity' and 'decorum' demand VIP treatment, for this is no 'proletarian slouch' and the saecular songs were 'decked out in the bluest of blue-blood' (vv. 66, 97, *neque plebeiam ~ patricio . . . ostro*). Two reasons why Apollo can 'unroll' the book of Gallicus' *Roman Life* (v. 80, *quid . . . reuoluam*, rewriting the spinning of Clotho, v. 2, uolu*it opus*, as re-reading). Apollo presents his apprentice son with a poetically touched-up *Life of Rutilius* to inscribe the Prefect's worth and sanction theurgy ('encomium', v. 85, *laudem*).

Why is Apollo so nervous about tempting fate? To underline that Laws aren't there to be broken, they make the world go round? Ask the Chief of Police! To emphasize how much Rome cares for her own? What a big deal Statius' little poem wants to be.[162] How precarious human life and occasional lyric both are and shall stay!

Apollo's litotes opened a telling gap, for his (inspired) poetry to fill, and for his peroration to close: 'no plebeian soul' (v. 66). He does his best. Rattling off his write-up of the Gallicus biography (*Vita*), he packs more than he can squeeze into his dash through the time-warp to the emergency ward (vv. 67–8, 80–93, 'just as briefly as this, while we come up to his home . . . Why need I unfurl . . .? What point in praise from me . . .? No room for . . . epics to open wide'). No. He may be Apollo, but he can't do justice to this promising theme: Gallicus needs and feeds an epic, and *Siluae* are supposed to be short poems. As Callimachus learned from Homer's hymns, when he sang *his* song of *Apollo*, *hymns* find their own way to deliver grandness, by protesting their feebleness in the face of their material (so easy to sing Apollo, so hard not to fail to sing him well!).[163] A hymn comes on as a 'prelude', living up to its billing *by* witnessing that it cannot: turns refusal into humility, reluctance into devotion, short weight into amplification!

No time to lose, or it will be too late for Gallicus (this is a 'snatch', a last-dash raid to hi-jack Gallicus from Fate, v. 94). Yet Apollo will treat his peroration with kid-glove circumspection, staying just, vitally, piously, short of *guaranteeing* success:

[1] 'If what I say is no disgrace' (v. 94) suspends the declaration, opening a new gap with its condition(al), even as it risks and avows self-confutation: for 'we shall snatch from the foul play / of Jupiter' is no way to teach a son respect for a father, even if it does dare the future indicative guarantee. This 'if' isn't going away.[164]

[2] 'For it was not in vain that . . .' (v. 95, *neque . . . frustra*) actually re-imports equivocation (along with litotes). Even as Apollo specifies what Domitian, the *pater patriae*, 'has earned' as 'what he is praying for' (vv. 95f., *rogat hoc . . . / et meruit*), he opens a gap between the performative acceptance of obligation, and mere gratitude for a generous tribute. Applause for the saecular hymn may *or may not* imply some sort of recognition of indebtedness, the terms depending on what strings exactly were attached to the prayers offered up, but it falls well short of obligating Apollo to flout *his* (better not to say it, but there it is)—tyrant.[165]

This is indeed the nub of the entire ensemble of prayerful caution— 'threading' the text together.[166] Apollo replicates at the divine level the fix of the thanksgiving poem from below. On the conditionality of Apollo's 'if' (viz., the reception of his avowedly encomiastic rhetoric as a 'just' description), the transcendence of Jupiter's power must, in the final reckoning, authorize the cure. Jupiter *cannot* be bound to any obligation, and 'stay of execution from busily-spinning Fate' is only his to grant. Not for son Apollo to 'set to, and make a grab for the distaff'! (vv. 63f.) His future indicative (re)assurance to *his* son, 'No need to fear that black-out / thunderbolt, Jupiter will approve this use of our art out loud' (vv. 64f.), was all bluff, as the iron fist in this velvet glove shows straight through the blithe self-confidence: if this can sound like an open *guarantee*, it could have no power to authorize the raid, and couldn't save either of the daring duo from the retribution so glaringly paraded in denial: his jussives (vv. 63f., 65, *teneamus . . ., ne . . . sit*) come from a father, they can't bind a father, let alone *the* Father. In fact, Apollo's promise contains within itself the admission that Jupiter is, like any emperor, a law unto himself: what he does will *always* be done 'off his own bat' (v. 65, *ultro*, 'going further than need be').

What Apollo is about is jollying Jupiter along, making what amounts to an indirectly voiced plea sound as if supreme self-confidence gets you everywhere. Once you get right down to it, he is 'talking up a storm' here; or, rather, he is 'softening steel with *his* civil politesse',[167] using oratory to exorate the inexorable, and orate it into being 'not inexorable' (v. 1). The 'use of our art(s)' he mentions here refers, of course, primarily to the medical skill for which he claims—as non-specifically as possible—sanction (vv. 62ff., 'it falls to us . . . to resurrect a man', *datur . . . recreare uirum*), but Apollo is, of course, in the first place actually *practising* two of his other performing 'arts' as he speaks, *by* speaking here: he is pleading before Jupiter's tribunal, and he is creating poetry. He treats the end as uncontentious, 'grabbing the opportunity' with both pairs of hands available to him (v. 62). But look at his *laudatio* (*not* a *laudatio funebris!*): the best he can do is fancy/argue/soothe with his encomium of Gallicus. The litotes in the vaunt that the hero was 'not born without favour from godhead' (v. 66, *neque . . . dextro sine numine cretam*) rubs it in that this is one of those fragile 'creatures' born to die. But in the same gesture Apollo performatively vindicates the claim to divine protection: Gallicus *does* command 'divine consent' (*numen*='nod'), and *is* accompanied by 'divine favour' (*dextro . . . numine*), because *Apollo* is at his bedside. The long string of success through all the vicissitudes of Gallicus' *Vita* must confirm the assertion: which god would not want a part of the action?

'If' Apollo's cheek doesn't ruin everything, there's plenty to play for. If Jupiter approves the use of his arts, 'because' his son has such a silver tongue/writes such winsome verse, 'because' Gallicus is such a deserving case, 'because' Rome is such a loving city, 'because' Statius-Apollo are putting on such a good show, 'because' Domitian put on such a good show, or just 'because', this will reward the prayers of all of them, and demonstrate the *clemency* of Deathstiny (vs. v. 50). On the fate of one prayer rests the ensemble and the discourse of prayer.

A lot to rest on one presumptuous 'if'! Apollo's stream of assurances, each one playing between qualifications intersected with guarantees, clearly stems from anxiety. This is what it means to observe that his constatives 'deconstruct' around traces of difference and resistance. They betray the reason why he is summoned to lend his authority to the text, only to advert throughout his performance to the limitations on his power which are intrinsic to *his* divine status. Apollo is forever his father's son. He figures as qualification to the absoluteness/oneness/transcendence of deity, through the slippage inherent in the successiveness of paternity. The gap opened in *numen* between *superi* is a space where interplay between the power of a *Iup-piter* and an *Apollo* (son) can mould the pantheon as a system where law rules, but 'not inexorably', for exceptions might open to specially graceful pleading. Asking nicely enough, putting enough up front, pressing the right button, knowing the right people, can unlock any door. (To optimize chances, fire a versatile and elegant poet-laureate at an eternally and beautifully youthful favourite son.) Guess how the system of imperial Rome worked![168]

14

A *Roman Life*, on Paper:
vv. 68–93

... *'genus ipse suis permissaque retro*
nobilitas; nec origo latet, sed luce sequente
uincitur et magno gaudet cessisse nepoti.   70
prima togae uirtus illi quoque: clarus et ingens
eloquio; mox innumeris exercita castris
occiduas primasque domos et sole sub omni
permeruit iurata manus, nec in otia pacis
permissum laxare animos ferrumque recingi.   75
hunc Galatea uigens ausa est incessere bello
(me quoque!) perque nouem timuit Pamphylia messes
Pannoniusque ferox arcuque horrenda fugaci
Armenia et patiens Latii iam pontis Araxes.
quid geminos fasces magnaeque iterata reuoluam   80
iura Asiae? uelit illa quidem ter habere quaterque
hunc sibi, sed reuocant fasti maiorque curulis
nec permissa semel. Libyci quid mira tributi
obsequia et missum media de pace triumphum
laudem, et opes, quantas nec qui mandauerat ausus   85
exspectare fuit? gaudet Trasimennus et Alpes
Cannensesque animae, primusque insigne tributum
ipse palam laeta poscebat Regulus umbra.
non uacat Arctoas acies Rhenumque rebellem
captiuaeque preces Veledae et, quae maxima nuper   90
gloria, depositam Dacis pereuntibus Vrbem
pandere, cum tanti lectus rectoris habenas,
Gallice, Fortuna non admirante subisti.'

[1] . . . 'His family's one-man pedigree, his aristocracy is
a posteriori, and his origin isn't lost, but by the light that's
        come after
    is overcome and is glad of a mighty grandson to defer to.   70

[2] He too won civil excellence, first in line, as bright and massive
    in oratory. At once, in ops. at bases beyond count,
    in stations of sunset and early dawn, under every sun there is,
    the hand that took the oath saw service through, and peacetime
        stand-down, use of,
    permission denied, no let-up of adrenalin or gunbelt unbuckled.   75

[3] Galatia at its acme found nerve to go for him on their war-path
    (me, too!) and nine harvests on end he scared Pamphylia
    and Pannonian wildness, and fearful for artillery in tactical
        retreat
    Armenia, and the River Araxes, finally putting up with a
        Roman bridge.

[4] Why need I unfurl twin *fasces* and iterate jurisdiction over   80
    mighty Asia? Indeed Asia would willingly have herself three
        goes and more
    at him, but homeward calls the Official Calendar, and more
        than one promise
    of a bigger desk . . .

[5] . . . Take the miracle of tribute taxed from Libya,
    in full cooperation, a triumph crated back from a hot-bed of
        peace—what point
    in praise from me, vast riches not even the job creator was
        nerved   85
    to anticipate? Gladness for Trasimene and Alps
    and souls at Cannae, and first up for a badge-of-honour tribute,
    there was Regulus, in no uncertain terms, a ghostly ball of
        happiness large as life.

[6] No room for armies from the far north and the Rhine back to
        war
    and captive Veleda's curses, and—. . .   90

[7]   . . .—this the latest, and mother   90
    of all sagas—Rome in his safe-keeping during the Dacian
        massacre,

81

epics to open wide, that time the call came to take so great a
   driver's reins,
Gallicus, without a flicker of surprise from Fortune, and you
   took them up.'

[1] Statius' biography of Gallicus' *Roman Life* begins at the beginning, before the call of official honours.[169] Gallicus' ascendancy
has already defeated time (v. 68, *retro*). He is his family's real
founder, not because his/their origins were obscure, but because he
has eclipsed them. To know Gallicus is to know how *Q. Iulius
Cordinus* may overshadow *Rutilius Gallicus*; but it is also to know
that he truly is *Gallicus*, the senator risen to ennoble Turin, which
the poem just celebrated implicitly, with just enough obscurity for
us not to miss it (vv. 58f.). The 'victory won over his pedigree' is a
touch more of Apolline balm, as graceful 'yielding' by the
ancestors to descendants slips in a sweetener for Jupiter, not to be
provoked by grandson Aesculapius, but to permit him some
limelight, alongside his (A.'s) father / his (J.'s) son (see chapter 15).
Proving the point, *Gallicus* is how Statius and Apollo know him,
as distinctive a new name as '*Agrippa*' had once been: no need to
specify '*Rutilius*' (whether the metrically impossible *Rutili(us)*
scanned as: '∪ ∪ ∪ (. . .)', or the Ephesus stone's careful:
'*RUTĪLI(US)*: ∪ - ∪ (. . .)', as from Ov. *Fast.* 6. 563 onwards; see
chapter 1). Statius pictures Gallicus as a classic *parvenu* at the
capital, and bullishly proud of it (*domi nobilis*), leaving his origins
in his wake.[170] A one-man avalanche!

   Less dangerously, Gallicus matches Domitian's Flavians, whose
every acclamation similarly stressed their rise from nowhere
exalted to the 'Julian' mantle of *Caesar Augustus*:[171] Statius is even
quoting from Ovid's catasterism of Diuus Iulius: 'gazing down
from his twinkling star, he confesses that his son's services are
greater than his; glad to be mastered by him' (*Met.* 15. 850f., *stella
micat natique uidens bene facta fatetur / esse suis maiora et uinci
gaudet ab illo*). Wicked Ovid! Runs the conceit into the ground:
'The one whose wars, achievements at home and the hurtle of
material glory were less the agents of his metamorphosis into a
new constellation, the long-tressed star, than his offspring. For of
all the measures of Caesar none was a greater project than his
coming to be father to this man. Don't tell me there's more in
taming the British than siring so mighty a man!' (ibid. vv. 746–58).

[2] Gallicus' training for greatness is despatched with a decisive weighting to the military life. He *did* qualify for civil administration by rhetorical training in forensic oratory: his student gown came first, his official robes as City Prefect were the culmination (*toga*, vv. 71, 48).[172] If he was a 'bright' Apollo in class, he also promised heroic stature—in word as well as in name (v. 71, *clarus et ingens*, cf. v. 63: *Rutilius* means 'shining'; *Gallicus* suggests a Goliath of a 'Gaul'[173]). His intense, arduous and ubiquitous military career trained him in the hard school of Roman life.[174] He became the hand that took the imperial oath of allegiance,[175] the hand that fought the planet wide, for the peace allowed to others. It was all the same to our trooper, one front blurring into another, beyond count, just one tour of duty, 'all the way' (cf. vv. 74f., / per*meruit*, / per*missum*).

[3] But Statius does buckle down next, to pick out the highlights of Gallicus' service-honours, as listed in lapidary *Lives*. He has Apollo sketch the career of campaigns as a four-line mini-epic that recapitulates the imperial mission of Rome (see Figure 5c).[176] First weather 'vigorous aggression' (v. 76); then, through a 'gestation-period of terror' (v. 77), reap a harvest of 'subdued acceptance' (v. 79). As signalled (v. 73), this will be a Herculean globe-trotter's career, through Galatia, Pamphylia, Pannonia, Armenia, Asia, Africa, Alps, Arctic, Rhine, to Rome (vv. 76–91).[177] Can Statius get on paper the kudos that incision in marble and public display gives a *Roman Life*? Breathless Apollo certainly seizes his chance to bring out at length the 'geographical mobility' that created particular *Roman Lives*, where Gallicus in stone could only weave between service 'at home and abroad', in a double helix of magistracies and tours of duty, Rome and the provinces (chapter 1).[178] Statius for this once imagines a regimental cosmopolis!

Apollo starts his inspired flummery by pitting *Gal*licus against *Gal*atians, 'logically' enough. The whole idea of Italian Rome in the hands of a *Gallicus* under a *Germanicus* drips paradox. Are they best at dealing with threats to Rome because they beat the enemy at their own name?[179]

At once the Celtic Galatians' raid westwards through the Greek world (279/8 BCE), all the way to ransack Apollo's Delphi, is sweetened into the sort of tantrum from a feisty nymph Apollo has to put up with (*Galatea* is the beloved of Cyclops),[180] and *lightened* into the tiniest parenthetic concession (v. 77, 'and on me, too', *(me quoque)*). Apollo pretends that the Roman occupation of the province of Galatia was more like resisting the Galatian Huns than fighting off the nymphette! Her sister *Pam*, better known as *Pamphylia*, at once finds Gallicus the sort of threat Apollo constitutes for nymphs, and she is joined by her twin *Pan . . . nonius*, and the rhyming twosome-in-one-verse / Arm*enia . . . patiens* and po*ntis* Ar*axes /*. The famous 'Parthian shots' fired by cossacks in retreat (pretended? You could never tell) have been countered, terror faced down by terror (at least they were on the run?), as Gallicus sets about settling the threats on Horace's agenda for (his) Augustus.[181] He has completed the Roman mission, too, by putting the last rivet in the bridge across the River Araxes which Virgil left to be the very last 'rivet' in the Shield of Aeneas: as Caesar Augustus celebrated his triple triumph, consecrated his immortal vow to the gods of Italy, the whole city explodes in 'joy and games', with massive sacrificial offering; the master sits on the 'snowy threshold of shining Phoebus' to receive tribute from a captured cosmos, that culminates in the 'now gentler Euphrates', etc., etc., and finally, 'Araxes affronted by its bridge' (*Aen.* 8. 714–28, pon*tem indignatus* Araxes. //). So Gallicus has now reconciled the River with its bridge too far, and got Armenia 'used to its Latin lesson: *pons, pontis*, masculine, third declension' (= v. 79!).[182]

[4] As peace erupts, Gallicus' round of assignment upon assignment culminates in governorship of Asia. He has re-doubled spell or spells of command there to his credit: the province would love yet more return-visits, but duty meantime recalled Gallicus to Rome, for another repeat tenure, a second term of higher magistracy (cf. v. 80, re*uoluam*). The Good Soldier Gallicus's life is one tale of 'permission' granted/denied, army-fashion (vv. 68, 75, 83). Now the Hun has scarpered, and the eastern front is pacified, the empire can relax: princess Asia would love to have this beau some more, just her kinda man (vv. 81f.).[183] Alas, duty 'calls', home tugs him away (v. 82, *revocant fasti*)![184]

[5] 'Miracles of submissive courting' now flow, a 'tribute of affection in a mountain of presents', as the circle from insolent, giganto-machesque, vandalism is closed in 'volunteered outbreak of peace

and spontaneous celebrations of Roman rule!' (= v. 84, souped up!). 'Beyond the wildest dreams of the one who made the appointment' (from v. 76, *ausa est* to v. 85, *ausus*). Yes, Gallicus' effort bestows upon the Empire, 'world-wide' (v. 73), 'the civilized peace' of Roman Life (v. 71, *togae*, v. 74, *otia pacis*). When Apollo is done, Gallicus' mission to run tax-gathering in the province of Africa has crowned centuries of imperial history. As if in response to epiphany of Apollo, the miracle occurs, a spontaneous outpouring of tribute. Africa's own thanksgiving, for belonging to Gallicus' Rome.

Statius winds back Roman history to the start of the Roman imperial adventure beyond Italy. Gallicus' exploits in the east and south finally bring joyful culmination to the legacy of the Republic. At the end of his catalogue comes vindication for the 'first-and-foremost' hero whose shade still awaits reparation from his descendants: *primus . . . Regulus* (vv. 87f.). At last came the special mark of acclaim which another Roman bi-consular, M. Atilius *Regulus*, that 'Prince-ling' of service to Rome, had long 'demanded'. Ever since, in history, the First Punic War, and in lyric, ever since Horace's fifth *Roman Ode*, where the mission of (any) 'Augustus' to extend the Empire as vice-gerent on earth of *Iuppiter Tonans* turns at once to the crusade of cleansing stains of repulsion and disaster from the annals. In outrage at the degradation of captive Romans who have capped their surrender and forgot themselves in 'oblivion of Italy, Rome, imperial Eternity, while Jupiter and the City survive' (vv. 9–12), the priest-poet animates the dead hero who died in obedience to *his* oath to return to Carthage, for execution after dissuading parley.[185] Finally, Gallicus 'answers happy Regulus' prayers, pays the debt which "Regulus" means for Rome' (= vv. 87f.). And Apollo spreads happiness all the way from Rome to Hell (v. 88, cf. 13, 123), for this moment reverses Lucan's Underworld scene, where patriots are grim, except for Brutus enjoying the prospect of Caesar's assassination, and the revolutionaries are 'gleeful' (6. 784–92, 793–6, . . . lae*tantis . . . Drusos*).

In Apollo's hands, the threads of Gallicus' career respond to all the calls for atonement which unite Graeco-Roman victims of barbarian humiliation: Asia Minor and the Delphic navel of the Earth, at Galatian hands; Italy and the World centered on Rome, at Gallic and Punic hands. Regulus' self-sacrifice led to victory in the First Punic War, which brought Hannibal's Carthaginians to invade Italy from the north. Shades of Gallic invasions across the *Alps*, Hannibal brought massacre to Roman soldiers and disgrace to Roman souls at Lake *Trasimene* and, worse massacre still, *Cannae*. Undoing the work of Hannibal gives countless ancestors satisfaction—hosts of soulful prayers answered (vv. 86f.). You could say Gallicus' career hunted down the legacy of Hannibal to the bitter end, all over again, for Hannibal fled off to the east for his last stand with Antiochus the Great, last ruler of *Asia* before the Roman Conquest, then fresh defeat off *Pamphylia*, and final incursion to the Aegean seaboard with Prusias of Bithynia against the Roman protectorate of Pergamum—in the tracks of the *Galatians*.

[6] Apollo won't (can't?) dwell on the northern front. Enough, where Virgil wrote, of the great Marcellus, *sternet Poenos Gall*umque rebellem / (*Aen.* 6. 858, 'He shall flatten Carthaginians and up-rising Gaul'), for Statius to up-date with . . . *Rhen*umque rebellem / ('v. 89, up-rising Rhine').[186] Germany spells, for Apollo, just one more poor 'captivated female begging for it', a rival priestess for his Sibyl, taught to pray to Rome for forgiveness, not to curse Rome with damnation.[187] Statius would love us to picture Gallicus bringing a northern Medea/Cleopatra to Rome in chains.

[7] Apollo introduces his last neglected epic theme as (and with) the climax, through the displayed echo of Virgilian Evander's climax to his aetiology for the hymnal celebration of the foundation of Rome's Greatest Altar (*Ara Maxima*): 'We'll call it always the Greatest of Altars, and it will always be the Greatest' (*Aen.* 8. 271f., *quae maxima semper / dicetur nobis et erit* quae maxima *semper* /). Statius effortlessly intimates that Domitian's recent annihilation of the Dacians had to feel like the re-foundation of Rome, and another giant Cacus throttled by the Flavian Hercules. Dacia was another outstanding score on the Augustan slate settled by this Germanicus (e.g. Hor. *Carm.* 3. 6. 14, 3. 8. 18): where Horace wrote 'Only special people can put "The Dying Gaul" into writing' (Hor. *Serm.* 2. 1. 13f., *pereuntis . . . Gallos*), Flavians could boast: 'Dateline: "The Dying Dacians"' (v. 91, *Dacis pereuntibus*).

Boss and protégé close ranks here: 'no miracle here, nothing left to chance' (v. 93, *Fortuna non admirante*, cf. 6: Fortuna *hated* this). The officer is finally brought back from the field to Rome, 'charged with Rome's safe-keeping'. He is the 'Chosen One', as close to the great Chooser as *lectus* is to *rector* (v. 92). So close that Palace-Watchers could not fail to detect Apollo virtually tipping Gallicus as 'The One Most Likely To Succeed'. When Statius shows us the apostrophized Prefect 'taking up / undergoing the reins of so great a driver', we can see him as: Domitian's donkey, still (cf. v. 6); in the driver's seat on the triumphal chariot that rolled along the Sacred Way up to bring spoils to Capitoline Jupiter *Optimus Maximus*; and/or stand-in for the emperor, deputizing while Domitian was away at the front. So near, yet so far!

Apollo knows better than to divert encomium from the emperor's Dacian triumph onto a cramped lyric for Gallicus, for Statius had devoted his (lost) *On the Dacian War* to that theme.[188] He reins the poem in with two metaphors that activate Gallicus' special commission to play caretaker of Rome: 'no room to open wide (the repressed themes)' fits him as ever-vigilant soldier-and-untiring-Prefect, and as gate-keeper of Rome (vv. 89, 92, *non uacat . . . pandere*).[189] Enter Domitian, rising still higher above his elevated minionster, as 'The famed Father of the City' (v. 95). Domitian the High Priest whose prayers must count with the Almighty Jove, the transcendent Father. Myth here begins again to think through the positions of Domitian and Gallicus by displacement to both Jupiter and Apollo, and to Apollo and Aesculapius. Paternity and therefore legitimized heredity lurk hereabouts, all but pencilling-in one Prefect where a son-and-heir for Germanicus should be. For the saecular procession that wends its way from Apollo's Palatine up to Jupiter's Capitol precisely honours the Almighty as 'Father'. We have now seen a whole raft of considerations that suggest Apollo's laudation of Gallicus' Roman Life must risk stirring outrage from 'Unfair Jupiter' (vv. 94f.).

15

Apollo's Pharmacy:
vv. 98–105

'*siqua salutifero gemini Chironis in antro*
herba, tholo quodcumque tibi Troiana recondit
Pergamus aut medicis felix Epidaurus harenis   100
educat, Idaea profert quam Creta sub umbra
dictamni florentis opem, quoque anguis abundat
spumatu: iungam ipse manus atque omne benigne
uirus odoriferis Arabum quod doctus in aruis
aut Amphrysiaco pastor de gramine carpsit.'   105

'Anything in twin Chiron's health-bearing cave,
any herb; whatever Troy's Pergamum stores in your
rotunda; or Epidaurus' blessed spa on the beach   100
educates in her nursery; the one Crete has carpet the shade of Ida,
bloom of dittany's potency; and the snake's spate of
spit . . .—I can apply dexterity, plus every kindly
poison that in Arabia's scent-prolific fields the learnèd
shepherd gathered me, or else from the sward of Amphrysus'.   105

Gallicus' resuscitation is a soteriology for Apollo, for Aesculapius, for
Domitian, for Gallicus, for Rome: bringing saecular revival and salvation
renewed, eternity and poetry. Apollo's intercession in response to
Domitian's plea traces from the offering of the *carmen saeculare*. The
charming sing-song of Statius' miniature evocation bridges and blurs into
the hocus pocus of Apollo's brew of potions: *this carmen* ('spell/song/
poem') has told us to LISTEN, as it spells out music, the healing force of
the universe (*carmina . . . sonuistis*, 'the sound of music', v. 97).

Rhyme doubles, rhythm redoubles hexameters, into a couplet of lyrical evocation:

```
-  UU    - UU - ‖  UU-    U U- U   U   - -
```
carmina *patricio,* *pueri,* *sonuisti*s in *ostro.*
[Songs; patrician;   ‖   boys; you sounded; in the purple]

```
-  U    U - UU -  ‖ U U -       - - U    U   - -
```
siqua *salutifero* *gemini* *Chironi*s in *an*tro
[any; health-bearing ‖ twin Chiron; in the cave]

The internal rhymes of nouns at verse end with their polysyllabic adjectives at the main caesura, the rhymes between the first feet in both 'halves' of the twinned verses and the emphatic parallelism in the cadences of the last two pairs of feet import the magic of choral bestowal of 'honour'. Children (boys doubled inclusively with girls) 'dressed in Roman purple match offspring to symbolic parentage' (*patricio, pueri*). These hexameters do more than cite Horatian lyric—they recite a dash of it.

Pharmacology resounds in the cave acoustics of its musical master, the centaur Chiron.[190] This 'miscegenate' (*gemini*) is a *positive* monster, as his verbal equivalent, the compound epi/thet 'health-bearing' (*saluti/fer-*), takes care to ensure. This is the classic lyric vision from Pindar: 'Deep-cunning Chiron reared Jason in his rocky home, and later Asklepios, whom he taught the soft-handed régime of drugs' (*Nem.* 3. 53ff.). After the god has ransacked his cosmos for medicaments to stir into his panacea *carmen,*[191] he encircles his effort within a magical echo:

```
-  UU    - UU-  ‖ UU -    UU - U   U   - -
```
carmina patricio,   *pueri,* *sonuistis* in *ostro.* /
[Songs; patrician;   ‖   boys; you sounded; in the purple]

```
-  U    U - UU-  ‖  U U -     - - U   U   - -
```
siqua *salu*tifero *gemini* *Chironis* in *an*tro /
[any; health-bearing ‖ twin Chiron; in the cave]

herba . . . *. . .* quodcumque *. . .* *. . . recondit* /
[herb . . .   . . .   whatever . . . . . . has hidden] (vv. 97–9)

... omne *benigne* /

[... one and all, kindly]

‑ U U ‑ U U ‑   ‖ U U ‑   ‑   ‑ U U . ‑ ‑
uirus odoriferis   Ar*abum quod doctus* in *aruis* /

[poison; scent-bearing;‖ Arabs'; which skilled in the fields]

-U U ‑   ‖
aut Amphrysiaco   ...   gramine   carpsi   .   //

[or; from Amphrysus; ‖ . . . green, I plucked.'] (vv. 103–5)

This sorcerers' phonic brew is going to (its 'double, double, toil and trouble') work, too:

... *monstrantque   simul   parentque   uolentes* /

[. . . They gesture and at once they obey with a will]

‑UU ‑ ‖ UU‑   U U ‑ U U   ‑ ‑
donec   letiferas   uario   medicamine   pestes /

[until; death-bearing ‖ with manifold medication; plague]

... *somni* /

[. . . sleep]

... *omni* /

[. . . all] (vv. 108–11).

Pull out all the stops, Gallicus deserves heap good medicine. Between Chiron and his translation *manus* ('hand-s', vv. 98 <> 103),[192] we must hunt for all the Prefect's worth, in herbal reckoning, from a 'learnèd' catalogue display (v. 104, *doctus*). Gallicus is . . . unique as the *hapax legomenon* that reclaims him, the serpents' stream of *spumatu* (v. 103 'spittle': copious as Gallicus' eloquence, vv. 102 <> 35, *abundat/as*).[193] At the other extreme, reference to the Virgilian battlefield where dittany is divinely procured for Aeneas' poison-dart wound is on display for our Old Soldier. A correctly 'Paeonian-girt' physician or two perform the surgery once again, just as Apollo's pupil Iapyx had (unknowingly) been aided by Aeneas' mother Venus, who 'plucked dittany from Cretan Ida, verdant in bloom, and sprinkles on the sap of ambrosia to bring health' and slipped it in the dressing (*Aen.* 12. 400–19, *ille retorto* / Paeon*ium*

*in morem . . . suc*cinctus *amictu . . . dictamnum . . . Cretaea* carpit ab
Ida, / . . . flore comantem *. . ., spargitque salubris / ambrosiae sucos et*
odoriferam *panaceam*).[194] Myth here translates Gallicus into as stoical a
national war-hero as the Empire could ever have seen since the
beginning.

Before cropping dittany and venom, Apollo ransacked his son's chief
storehouses, at 'Trojan Pergamum' and Epidaurus (cf. v. 61, 'my child
from Epidaurus'). The Empire's global system of cults permits Apollo
and Asclepius to team up. Perhaps the greatest gift of the Flavian
dynasty to Roman piety was investment in the Sanctuary of Asklepios
Soter ('Saviour') at Pergamum.[195] Here you will find Statius (in *Silu.* 3.
4) dedicating Domitian's favourite, Earinus', locks, after he became,
thanks to Aesculapian surgery, the last subject to lose his *bol*locks
before his master had castration barred from the Empire. In Pergamum,
within his 'rotunda' that stood for the earth, 'the mild god sleeps in,
with health-bearing snake' (*Silu.* 3. 4. 25). At this Temple, the hymns

Figure 7.   Asklepios, on coin of Epidaurus (*LIMC* II. 1, Asklepios 84:
Moulage Winterthur Stadtbibliothek Phot. *LIMC*).

started from the story of Telephus, instantly cured by Achilles' wounding spear (vv. 112f.). Of course 'battling Machaon's juicy salve for Menelaus'—originally produced by Chiron (cf. v. 98) and handed down from Asclepius to *his* son—is Pergamene as well (vv. 113f.); and, in a sense, the same goes for the recreation of Trojan Aeneas by Iapyx' dittany (vv. 101f.).

In Pergamum, as at the Delphi-accredited centre of the cult, Epidaurus (Figure 7), and in Rome, Asclepius' pilgrims were treated to divine healing by dreams/epiphanies during 'incubation', as well as by the laying on of hands (cf. v. 103),[196] and the range of more or less drastic interventions (cf. *uario medicamine*, v. 109, with Pind. *Pyth.* 3. 47–54). Some cures were miraculous visions; others good healthy regimen. The course for Gallicus calls for herbs plus massage: hence the poet's prayer will prove to be to *Apollo Thymbraee* (v. 117), the local Pergamene deity from Thymbra in the Troad, named for *thumbra*, 'savory' or 'thyme'—a lowly seasoning for a pious Silvan sacrificial serving. It was to this cult that Virgilian Aristaeus' prayer referred for the name of his father when his swarm needed raising from the dead ('If my father is indeed Apollo of Thymbra', *Georg.* 4. 323, *si . . . pater est Thymbraeus Apollo*).[197] In a saecular hymn, *mitis Apollo* ('mild Apollo') is honoured (along with his twin sister) by commemoration of Trojan origins as the power of Roman piety (Hor. *Carm. Saec.* 33f.; 37–50).

(Unmetrical) Aesculapius was summoned to Rome itself from Epidaurus, by Sibylline order, to mop up a plague. He settled cheek-by-jowl with father's father, Jupiter, on the tiny asylum of Tiber Island, and came first in every Roman calendar (Ov. *Fast.* 1. 294, 'the grandson's temple adjoining grandfather').[198] To write up an Asclepian *Iama* ('Inscription of a Miracle Cure')[199] in Rome, as Statius shows, serves to glorify and propitiate Apollo. And to play off the sacred tale of their own tussle with inexorable Fate.

In the Graeco-Roman story of *Vir/bius* ('the mortal who lived twice, *vir+bis*', and 'the hero of life, *heros+bios*)', 'mild Asclepios' (*epios Askl/epios, mitis deus*[200]) was punished for reviving dead Hippolytus by being blasted by Jupiter's bolt: as Ovid winds up his half-baked Calendar of Roman Life, with Aesculapius returning at the death, *Clotho* (cf. v. 1) is pained that 'the threads be re-spun' (*Fast.* 6. 757, *fila reneri*; cf. vv. 7, 64, *fila, fila*).[201] In retaliation, Apollo shot up the Cyclopes to halt further production of thunderbolts (cf. v. 64);

reconciliation with his favourite son meant grandfather Jove had to restore grandson Aesculapius to more than life—to 'divine status' (ibid. 761, *deus est*).[202] The Almighty was thus forced to do precisely what he had made an example of Aesculapius for doing: 'he did what he banned from being done' (ibid. 762). But this scalp for Asklepios is not the half of it.

Statius displays by quotation the intrication of his *soteria* with Ovid's deployment of Aesculapius in his not-so-brief history of time, the *Metamorphoses*: 'he took his son into the cave of twin Chiron and Chiron's daughter prophesied: "Grow, child, health-bearing to the whole world"' (2. 542–675 (Coronis), esp. 629f., 642f., *natum* . . . geminique *tulit* Chironis in antr*um* /, . . . 'toto . . . salutifer *orbi* / *cresce puer*') ~ 'in twin Chiron's health-bearing cave' (v. 98, salutifero gemini Chironis in antro /). When serpentine Aesculapius comes to Rome, and brings the narration to Rome, 'he came bringing health to the city' (15. 622–744, *uenitque* salutifer *Urbi*). He turns out to be, and turns into, Ovid's example of the 'alien' (*aduena*) who models for the Caesarian apotheosis 'in his own city' (745–851).[203] As we saw in chapter fourteen, Statius wrote Ovid's naughty glorification of Diuus Augustus at the expense of Diuus Julius into his account of Gallicus' own retroactively glorified pedigree, just after Apollo reminded us how resuscitation of Gallicus would put himself and his 'Epidaurian child' into jeopardy again with (grand)father Jupiter (vv. 70, 61–5).

The logic of Statius' pharmacopoeia of myth is that Gallicus ahould play Hippolytus/Virbius to Domitian's Aesculapius; but Gallicus plays Aesculapius, too, to the afflicted of Rome, satellite of Domitian's Apollo; and Gallicus is imperial 'Apollo' as well, to Domitian's Jupiter ('Father of Rome', v. 95). Apollo accordingly must switch between the 'Apollo' and 'Jupiter' roles. And Domitian modulates between 'Jupiter', 'Apollo' and 'Aesculapius'. All but coming into view is the emperor's own heroic crisis between temporary guise of mortality and his destined translation to eventual divinity (following his father and brother).

If the reconciliation of Jupiter to Justice restores peace to an amplified family of gods, that is at the inexorable price of a comically self-betraying U-turn from the Almighty. Such is the structural double/bind of polytheistic dissemination. Lines of power run, tangle and split, through the poem: *superi-sidera-di-fila-Fata-Aoniae diuae-astra-orsa-fila-di-sidera-fila-sorores-di*; as against the integrative forces: *Clotho-caelum-Fortuna-Fatum-Fortuna*; personalized roles import further authority and raise questions for authority: *Astraea-Iuppiter-Phoebus-Pallas-Tegeae Dircesue alumnus-Gallicus-Ceres-Lyaeus-Diana-Bellipotens-luna-deus Apoll[o]-Epidauria proles* [Aesculapius]-*Iuppiter-Iuppiter-Chiron-pater uatum Thymbraee* [Apollo].To turn this round, classical myth is a supple medium for exploring the complexities of our several and collective temporalities.[204]

Apollo ends his speech by further signalling its poisonously curative balm in terms of unspoken but insistent discord within the divine order, when Apollo *Nomios* was sentenced to servile work, for Admetus, as 'herdsman from the green of Amphrysus' (v. 105) ~ 'herdsman from Amphrysus', Virg. *Georg.* 3. 2, / *pastor ab Amphryso*, culled from 'When once at Amphrusos . . .', Callim. *Hymn* 2. 48, / *exot' ep' Amphrussôi* . . .[205] Understanding *this* item culled from the exotic 'fields' of Apolline poetics perhaps calls most insistently for 'learning', for here Statius vaunts his omnivorous 'culling' of all the Graeco-Roman supply of benign curatives, to produce a renewal of *poetry*.

16

Take Up Thy Bed, and Walk:
vv. 106–14

. . . *inueniunt positos iam segniter artus*
pugnantemque animam; ritu se cingit uterque
Paeonio monstrantque simul parentque uolentes,
donec letiferas uario medicamine pestes
et suspecta mali ruperunt nubila somni.   110
adiuuat ipse deos morboque ualentior omni
occupat auxilium. citius non arte refectus
Telephus Haemonia, nec quae metuentis Atridae
saeua Machaonio coierunt uulnera suco.

. . . They find his limbs by now slackly sprawled
and his soul making a stand. Both gird themselves in the ceremonial
    style
of Paeon and together they gesture and they obey with a will,
until death-laden plague, versus manifold medication,
and coma's glowering cloudbanks of sick sleep were shattered by
    them.   110
The patient helps the gods and more than a match for any affliction
he gets in before help comes. No swifter a revival by
Haemonian skill was Telephus', nor panicked Menelaus'
raw wounds knitting through Machaon's elixir.

Statius invents a lively little scene, of bustling teamwork—like Darby
and Joan.[206] Apollo *Medicus* & Son match word to deed, break speed-

records ('He stopped. They find; each girds himself; they gesture and obey all at once', vv. 106ff.). Instant expert appraisal: 'limbs slack= death-struggle'.[207] How well these gods understand human fragility, a soul and his body are soon parted (cf. vv. 54–6)![208] They are gods, too (for all that they sport our operating gowns). Apolline sunshine through Gallicus' clouded spirit (v. 110), they are 'benevolent' answer to any casualty's prayers.[209] Yet the gods help those who help themselves, and Gallicus' lightning rally is down to his own inner strength, his ('007') never-say-die attitude.[210] A miracle cure for this military man, military recovery for a military fatigue: 'his recovery is as swift as Statius' allusions to Virgil and Horace can make it'![211] The heroes of Homeric epic were comparative slow-coaches: 'Telephus revived by Haemonian skill' was healed by the rust of Achilles' spear that wounded him; and 'the raw wounds of Menelaus, son of Atreus, by Machaon's sap'.[212]

Not dead, just Asclepe!

17

It Takes a Worried Man to
Sing a Worried Song:
vv. 115–22

quis mihi tot coetus inter populique patrumque 115
sit curaeque uotique locus? tamen ardua testor
sidera teque, pater uatum Thymbraee, quis omni
luce mihi, quis nocte timor, dum postibus haerens
adsiduus nunc aure uigil, nunc lumine cuncta
aucupor; immensae ueluti conexa carinae 120
cumba minor, cum saeuit hiems, pro parte furentes
parua receptat aquas et eodem uoluitur austro.

What space among all these gatherings of the Roman people and
    Fathers, 115
could there be for my prayerful care? Yet I call to witness the
    towering
stars and you, from Thymbra, father of bards, what all through
the daylight, all night, was the fear I felt, while clinging to the
    doorway
in twenty-four hour surveillance, varying ear with eye, I staked out
the lot, just as when, on tow from an aircraft-carrier, 120
a tiny dinghy, once the storm rages, takes its proportion of raving
waters, scaled down, and rolls under the same sou'wester.

All in the same moment of ritual time, Statius gathered the thronging
metropolis to pray for Gallicus, 'senators, equestrians, plebeians'

(vv. 39f., *patrumque equitumque . . . et plebis*), zipped through the supernatural jump-start, and now buttons on his own puny vow: 'my prayerful care among all these gatherings of the Roman people and their Fathers, the Senate' (vv. 115f., *coetus inter populique patrumque . . . curae uotique*). He mediates relations between the citizens and their officer, and between Apollo and his poets (both Gallicus and our poet).[213] Channelled through him, as figure for the small but pure modality of lyric poetry, is a supplementary commitment of personal prayers, vow, and affect.[214] His appeal to the stars, untiring attendance on the door round the clock, catching at all possible clues, at once performs *cura*, from a client / loving friend, and a guard's vigil.[215] The Callimachean poet and poem is 'a mere dinghy bobbing behind Gallicus' great galleon, the epic keel of state' (vv. 120–2).[216] Statius aboard his sieve, *Silu.* 1. 4, makes heavy weather of it, as this roughed-out minor poem improvised by the laureate of oceanic epic construction 'rides its storm, ships heavy seas, and rolls alarmingly in its teacup of poetic tempest' (vv. 121f.).

18

Many Happy Returns:
vv. 123–31

nectite nunc laetae candentia fila, sorores,
nectite, nemo modum transmissi computet aeui:
hic uitae natalis erit. tu Troica dignus 125
saecula et Euboici transcendere pulueris annos
Nestoreique situs. qua nunc tibi pauper acerra
digna litem? nec si uacuet Meuania ualles
aut praestent niueos Clitumna noualia tauros
sufficiam. sed saepe deis hos inter honores 130
caespes et exiguo placuerunt farra salino.

Twine the thread to a sheen! Be glad now, sisters,
Twine on, let none reckon the limit of time passed!
Today will be the birth-day of his life. You are worth it: Trojan 125
aeons and the years' heap of Euboean dust, Sibyl,
and of mouldered Nestor. With what incense-bowl should my
    humble self now
gain you the propitiation you are worth? No, not if Mevania should
    empty her dales,
or Clitumnus' fresh-tilled fields afford snow-white bulls,
should I be enough. Though the gods have often, in the company of
    these offerings, 130
been won by turf and barley-meal, with just a shake of the salt
    cellar.

Terrorstruck prayers for those in peril on the sea give way abruptly to more exclamatory happiness! The 'moment' comes together here (*nunc*)! Statius begins a binding song that lulls the Fates into spinning more yarn, in a rhythmic chant that weaves on past the end of the verse to begin a new row, and warns that no one must keep a check.[217] And no one is to count up 'Aeons of the Past', in case 'twice six quinquennia', and reckoning of Gallicus' incipient 'old age', surface from bathetic recall of vv. 52f.

The poem 'rolls round the work' into a prayer-poem's ring-structure (v. 2),[218] to cure the end by procuring another beginning, for both Gallicus' life and Statius' text. To fix this as the day of re-birth for this Renaissance Man, Statius turns to epic hexameters from Rome's lyric genius, Catullus, and requests an encore from the Fates' marriage-hymn that pre-conceived the advent of Achilles in the final section of Catullus 64: 'soft threads of gleaming wool . . ., the sisters open for you on this joyous day . . ., speed on . . . speed on' (312–27, fila . . . candenti*s mollia lanae / uellera . . .* laeta *tibi pandunt luce* sorores . . . / *curr*ite . . . *curr*ite).

The poet-priest's universal jussive or optative subjunctive (v. 124) is followed by what could seem an authorizing assertion, 'This will be Day 1'; but in pragmatic terms, this assertion is a virtual apodosis, and we shall find that it speaks the boon a sacrificant means to bid for with his offering. So, *if* Fate obeys his imperatives, and *if* the whole of creation does what he tells them, *then* 'this will be the birth-day of his life' (v. 125).[219] From this point on, marks of conditionality and conation modify the constative force of this last outburst, so the finale will resume and resumé the entire *soteria*.

Appeal to 'worth' once again argues special treatment for deserving Gallicus (vv. 74, 94, 96, 125), as Statius at once breaks his own prohibition by 'computing the limits on exceptional life-spans in the past' (vv. 126, 124, / trans*cendere* ~ / trans*missi, computet* ~ *pulueris, aeui / ~ annos /*). Rating Gallicus above the 'Trojan aeons, the years of Cumaean dust' (vv. 125f.), counts for more than proverbial allusions to Priam, and/or Tithonus of Troy, and the Sibyl of Cumae, founded from Euboean Chalcis.[220] For we have been invited, in denial, to think over 'the past', and are bound to rehearse the line of Apolline Sibyls that have reasserted the foundation of Rome as the re-birth of Troy,[221] even as Graeco-Roman epic threads back through Virgil to Homer, with *his* (already) decomposed Nestor (v. 127). Gallicus deserves no less.

But an occasional lyric cannot presume to live up to so epic a hero: Statius moves into interrogative mood, appealing for help with his appeal (vv. 127f.). 'The moment of rejoicing' in theurgy (v. 123, *nunc laetae*) soon dissolves into the 'uncertain moment of prayer for propitious hearkening to prayer' (vv. 127f., *qua nunc . . . digna litem?*). This acolyte is alive to the question of his (in)adequacy to deliver what is needful, Gallicus' due. At the point of delivering the powers-that-be the tangible token of his thanks, he shears away into the formulae of self-deprecation. Certainty of material deficiency further cries up the measure of the beneficiary's worth. To make an end, the prayer subsides in asserting, for sure, that 'offerings have been known in the past to find favour with the gods'. But this faith in the efficacy of the 'widow's mite'—in Greek a 'cock to Asklepios'[222]—can only be asserted 'gnomically', as 'a far from uncommon occurrence' (v. 130, *saepe*).

On one side, Statius is sure that no offering *could* do justice to the Prefect. Loot Lucan or take what's on offer in Virgil's landscape, even perfection would not be enough. For 'Mevania's bull-bearing plains' and 'Clitumnus' bull, mightiest of sacrificial offerings, traditional supply for Roman triumphs' had—besides ill-serving as the Vitellian base against the Flavian forces in 69—featured in Lucan's first book, where Caesar emptied Italy of patriots, and in the *Georgics'* 'Praises of Italy' (1. 473; 2. 146–8).[223] On the other, Statius' recipé of 'crude instant altar, the ritual meal and salt for sacrificial sprinkling, along with generous prayer' dusts off that primeval humility that had for centuries 'found favour with the gods', as well as with the lyric poetry, that consecrated traditional *Roman Life*.[224] So: 'It worked *for* Horace', and 'It works *in* Horace—often'!

The pray-er must finally leave the space of the 'present moment' marked out as the gap between Rome and Divinity, the 'in-betweenness' of prayer. He has asked: 'What space could there be for my prayerful care among all these gatherings of the Roman people and their Fathers, the Senate?' (vv. 115f.). And, by the same token, he has found space for the Roman World and for Deathstiny in 'his modestly insufficient ditty'. If the brevity-celerity-humility of 'Statius' approach to writing songs of praise' (v. 130, *hos inter honores*) produces the refinement of Callimachean poetry, fit offering for the gods,[225] we should also recognize in it the lyric theme of Pindaric praise-poetry: *ars longa, uita breuis*.[226] The Appendix develops this in connection with the *soteria*. But next, two chapters will consider Gallicus' poem in the context of *Siluae* I.

101

19

It's the Thought that Counts:
Siluae 1. 4 and the *Preface*

Now cancer is thought of as a disease of the contamination of the whole world.[227]

Statius provides a prose *Preface* for the first gathering of a half-dozen *Silvae*, and this gives the poem on Gallicus a frame. The poem contributes its particular reflections to the larger ensemble, helping to fashion an entrée, on paper, to *Roman Life* at Domitian's court (see chapter 20). The *Preface* arranges to comment on each poem, guiding our surrogate reader in the text, the dedicatee Arruntius Stella, toward the project ahead. *Preface* mediates between poems and reader, proposing a perspective for their reception. But *Preface* and poems also interact, in particular staging a discussion of 'temporality'. Readers of the book can move back and forth between reading the poems as re-presentations of the occasions that motivated their composition, and reading the poems re-motivated as Statius' offering to his reading public. The *soteria* may turn out to embody very different concerns in the context of the book-collection than those presented by its one hundred and thirty odd verses. As in the case of the published lawcourt oration, or any other writing mounted as a dramatic script, prayers cannot record their own success or failure. A thanksgiving can only serve up what it purported to be about at the time; it cannot itself *tell* us what it is up to, what it always anticipated being for, what it is to do now. Re-presentation in a set of performances imports new considerations; but also brings out that the *soteria* all along meant more than it could say.

The opening sentence of the *Preface* at once prefixes the collection with staggered temporality:

diu multumque dubitaui[228] . . . *an hos libellos . . . congregatos dimitterem.*

I hesitated much, for ages: should I gather together these folios and put them out?

What a contrast with the celerity of their original individual production:

hos libellos, qui mihi subito calore et quadam festinandi uoluptate fluxerunt, cum singuli de sinu meo pro[—[229]

These folios which streamed from me in the heat of the moment and (how to put it?) that countdown thrill, when one at a time from my heart out they [—

There on the nose is the paradox of the writing of (all) the *Siluae*. There is no time for a full reading of the *Preface*, so we shall just nip through one or two of the main pointers that Statius took ages to agonize over! In these preliminaries, glosses on the individual poems will disclaim unity for the book; but the prefatory process of glossing will at the same time assert unity, around the issue of publication.

This book, he at once goes on to propose, will be Statius' equivalent of the *Culex* ascribed to Virgil's youth, or his *Batracho<myo>machia*, Homer's mock-epic skit. These folios will be this epic poet's after-the-event 'preludes' to his already published masterpiece, the *Thebaid* epic, whatever the actual relative priority of their writing may have been: 'how to let this gathering go its way', he puts it, when Statius is 'still afraid for his (darling) Thebaid, even though she's done gone and left me' (. . . *pro Thebaide mea quamuis me reliquerit*).

So *Preface* promotes for our immediate attention the question of temporality *within the poet's oeuvre*. *Siluae* from this bi-cultural Homer-and-Virgil-rolled-into-one, this Graeco-Roman classic, are given their place in his *Collected Works*. These are the personally-authorized, authenticated, definitive, *juvenilia* that any self-respecting and *soi-disant* 'illustrious poet' simply must have to his name—faked if necessary! Whether or not all or some of them were written before the epic was finished, or was finally released to a waiting world (as 1. 5 will be careful to claim for itself),[230] *Preface* gives us notice that the *Siluae* became an *opus* later—but are always to be re-inserted in editions to serve as introductory 'warm-up prelude' for the monumental volume to follow (*stilo remissiore praeluserit*). Statius' habit of carefully poising his work, begun with *Thebaid*'s deferential positioning in *Aeneid*'s train

(*Theb.* 12. 817), will develop through *Siluae Praef.* I into a sketch of his (terminal) writer's block with the second book of his second epic, *Achilleid*, which we should, accordingly, envisage as under production concurrently with various of *Siluae* IV and V (*Silu.* 4. 7. 23f.).

At every point, then, we Stellas must read Statius' 'lesser' poems in the light of his authorship of the great *Thebaid*. The luxuriant *folies* and *grandeurs*, the urbane Saturnalian facetiousness, of these lyrics, are made all the brighter for the agonized epic's implosive myth of the doomed anti-city of tragic suicide, plague, and meltdown.[231] The sparkle of the *Siluae* attests social cohesion and political order in contemporary Rome all the more emphatic for its juxtapositioning to the blocked and choked Oedipodonian rivalry and civil war in mythic Thebes. Yet the reflex must apply, too, and *Thebaid* undo Statius' Silvan Rome, as puerile 'prelude', a 'gnat' or 'battle of mice and frogs', a cross between mistake and pisstake. Relaxed *Siluae* are all the more relaxed (and flippant) for the hulking shadows of epic cataclysm; Rutilius Gallicus' devoted public service to eternal Rome speaks with all the greater resonance through Statius' epic authority.[232]

We are cued to the temporal shift from occasion to context in the book. Within the book as the unit of composition, the individual notice for 1. 4 makes a difference to the prayer for Gallicus that becomes in turn a function for the overall enterprise. *Preface* has the gall to 'heal' the thanksgiving poem's necessary lack of a final enunciation of the success of its prayers for Gallicus' return to health. As Statius runs through the six poems in sequence, he insists to our astonished incredulity that 'none of them dragged beyond forty-eight hours, some tipped out before the day was out'. His touts 'celerity' for his 'only plus point'. By adapting his variations on the formula to each poem, he fashions an opportunity to characterize them at a glance. The fourth shot goes:

> *sequitur libellus Rutilio Gallico conualescenti dedicatus, de quo nihil dico, ne uidear defuncti testis occasione mentiri.*

> Next in order, the poem dedicated to Rutilius Gallicus on the occasion of his recovery from illness. I make no mention of it, in case anyone should think I take the opportunity offered by the decease of a witness to tell lies.

Let's notice the precarious temporality in the inceptive *conualescenti* ('becoming strong again'), and the prefatory promise of full biographic treatment *ad hominem* (*de quo nihil dico*, 'I say nothing of his poem [until we reach 1. 4]'). Let's have a clumsy shot at spelling out the 'nothing' that we are here 'told' (beside the important, prosaic, information that the fourth poem's *Gallicus* will be *Rutilius*). We are keyed in to Gallicus as figure for 'sincere truth-telling' (*ne uidear mentiri*) in an encomium (*dedicatus*, 'dedicated') set within the ambience of the Law (*testis*, 'witness'). Let's savour in anticipation Gallicus, honoured champion of Flavian Law and Rome's Chief of Police. In charge of sub-poenas for witnesses, and investigator of death in suspicious circumstances and homicide (*defuncti testis occasione*, 'through the opportunity of the witness's death'). The poem is programmed to present its *Life of Gallicus* as affidavit, now *Preface* has promised 'under oath' that 1. 4 will tell the truth of Gallicus.

The *Preface* drops its poisonous news so lightly it may take you aback—or even entirely fail to register. The poem's joyous celebration of Gallicus' recovery from illness must turn to (the book's) sour cerebration of Gallicus' recovery from illness: *Gallicus is dead.*[233]

Doesn't that mean *Siluae* 1. 4 is past its sell-by date, too? Couldn't Statius bear to bury his posthumous ditty? Aren't we being told to dance on Gallicus' grave?[234]

Preface obliges readers to ponder the temporality of the *soteria*. If thanksgiving, as for recovery from illness, seems predicated on pastness—of cure, and so of illness[235]—the stagger between composition and collection has undone the logic as well as the realization of *that*. No. Thanksgiving is necessarily tied to the staging of a present ill, a precarious amelioration and an insistent *will* to put the crisis in the past. Thanksgiving is itself a dynamic occasion for prayer, structuring a charge of emotion between the occasioning blight and the representation which would cancel it. Thanksgiving is precisely bound to the recognition of *mortality*. This recognition is what it offers up to its gods in recompense for their aid. Constative assertiveness in the acclamation of recovery serves the performative goal of making the recovery *real*, preserving its course and so piloting it toward salvation. But such utterance must raise the question of its effectivity *as* its effectivity. It is just the way it is in court. Counsel's case cannot include the jury's verdict, but revolves around the mission of binding that verdict to its will: the oration imagines, disables, scotches all forms of pre-judgement it can anticipate, but can *never* at last show its case won, its will done. The *soteria* is another such scene, a 'pharmacological' scene we could call it, where the rhetorical project deconstructs into a baffled reach for its desired goal, or cure, and endless deferral through representation.[236]

The song that declares the recovery of the Flavian minister, Rutilius Gallicus, *wills* its telling of the recovery to achieve the recovery, to enact recovery by an assertion which would be proof against the very liability to relapse it must attest. The song wants to work as a spell which would deliver Gallicus to secure health. But the burden of its narrative of illness and alarm leading to solicitous prayers is not just the celebration of recovery, but rather the renewal of prayers for the survival of (exactly) the pious narrative of divine rescue, the structuring of a repetition. The curative power of the *soteria* resides in its fight against the constraints of mortality; the *soteria* enlists our desire to wish away those limits; and the *soteria* inscribes the need to draw their sting and soften their bite. But no prayer can defeat Deathstiny.

Preface makes sure to rub our noses in *that*. Yet the drama of trauma, devotion, offering does have a healing force. As the play of writing upon time, the *soteria* can be the celebration of (textual) *vivaciousness*. 1. 4 *has* saved *A Roman Life*. Gallicus is safe from obliteration, from oblivion, from inexorable temporality. Statius' own preservation cancels, precisely, the fatal threat of Gallicus' illness: 'forgetfulness of life' (v. 57).

For all the self-deprecation and polite humility it sports, the poem commemorates this *Life*, it *becomes* its inspiration, the living-dead Gallicus (vv. 19–37), who serves as the talisman of Rome, himself a 'kindly poison' that heals the *Life of Rome*. This gilded *Gaulois*, if poetry can detoxify poisonous fear, anxiety and fraction, is a saviour of 'saecular' renewal. If prayer always anticipates the potential for reversal of the reversal it implores, but can do no more than deprecate and deplore that possibility, nevertheless it provides an opening for communal solidarity. To demonstrate and celebrate caring, gratitude, congratulation just has to be good medicine.

So if the City Prefect's temporary reprieve didn't last long enough for Statius' instant hit-factory to dash out an album, that *needn't* deflate his song-and-dance. They would *all* be in their graves soon enough, but the precariousness of a *Life* written into prayer format was always a good bet for lacing encomium with readerly enjoyment. Especially between the covers of the world's greatest living poet, doing the honours. *Preface* makes dead sure we won't just join in the elation of 1. 4. That would be no way to remember iron man Gallicus. The Prefect books the sobriety of public service onto his page of *Roman Life*.

Statius' wicked rival Martial makes one of his good bad jokes out of all this (12. 56):

Aegrotas uno decies aut saepius anno,
  nec tibi, sed nobis hoc, Polycharme, nocet:
nam quotiens surgis, soteria poscis amicos.
  sit pudor: aegrota iam, Polycharme, semel.

Sick x 10 *per annum*, plus,
  and no harm to you, Polycharmus, only to us:
you see, every time you get better, you press friends for recovery
    pledges.
  For shame! get a grip and get sick, Polycharmus, just the once![237]

Brute history could play its own versions of the Gallicus trick. Even the
report of a 'recovery' could be temporary, as in 19, when the people
celebrated on the Capitol empty news of a rally by the dying
Germanicus (Suet. *Gai.* 6. 1). Again, a smart courtier could jump too
fast, as when Clutorius Priscus paid with his life when he pre-wrote a
lament for the imminently expected demise of the younger Drusus, who
promptly recovered (Tac. *Ann.* 3. 49f.). A canny prophet 'would
predict good health for the sick, but in case of fatality another oracle
was ready to recant this: "No more seek remedy for painful illness. /
For your fate clearly awaits and escape is not possible for you"' (Luc.
Alex. 42. 28). And the historian writing a history of historians could
court clammy prescience of mortality himself as he set himself 'the
problem of describing the . . . life of a distinguished contemporary and
social superior . . .', one that 'had not seriously been faced before'—
and news of the subject's decease arrived in mid-composition (Nep.
Att. 25. 19) . . .

   In the epistolary formula addressing the *Preface* to Stella, Statius
already brandished before us the keynote for the collection:

   Statius Stellae suo salutem

   Statius sends his own dear Stella all the best.

For *salus* extends from just the basic sociality of unvarnished 'greetings'
to the 'salvation' of Gallicus, and the 'security' of the state.[238] As a final
chapter will now indicate, the collection of *Siluae* I lays out a series of
six different studies of 'the point of existence'. Plenty for us Stellas to
mull over. Caught between *Preface* and poem, we must decide whether
Statius' Gallicus or his poem are to live or to die, whether to play
Apollo to his Asklepios, Aesculapius to his Hippolytus/Virbius.[239] Yes,
Gallicus lives?

20

The Sacred Wood:
Statius' Book of Etiquette (*Siluae* I)

> Should we attach symbolic significance to the fact that a fly never
> contracts typhus?[240]

Siluae 1 assembles six 'clips' from the world stretching before the likes
of Arruntius Stella. The cavalier emperor's new statue (1. 1), and his
restoration of the Capitol (1. 6. 101f.); the idyll of a holiday villa (1. 3),
the oasis of a brand-new bathing complex (1. 5); officially sponsored
Christmas fun-and-games (1. 6). A newly ennobled 'patrician' courtier[241]
must take to such blending of public roles with private interfacing as his
destiny. As earmarked consul-in-the-making and budding poet, Stella
will learn from Rome's poet-laureate of epic and lyric, as he contemplates empire and society, the flavour of life in cosmopolis:

[1] Stella was an insider in the pageantry of Domitian's saecular
games. Like his Augustan predecessor, the first senatorial and
consular Arruntius, and like the Flavian Arruntius Aquila, too,
Stella was with young Tacitus on the board of *XVuiri s[acris]
f[aciendis]* responsible for organizing this grandest of civil
tableaux (1. 2. 177).[242] Himself an elegist, Arruntius Stella can
star as Statius' version of Tibullus' Messalinus, the boy born for
the new age.[243]

[2] Stella will find himself already part of the social scene: his own
wedding celebrations promise renewal for *Roman Life* (1. 2).

So reading (t)his book-roll over Stella's shoulder presses us right into the norms and delights of Flavian Rome. Reading through the volume also overlays the individual pieces with a collective temporality beyond the terms of each. The poems frame each other by merging and 'bleeding' into their neighbours. Take a quick look at the intersections that affect (and constitute) 1. 4:

[1] The final part of 1. 3. wheels past us Vopiscus' *Pindaric* plectrum, his heroic lyre, his bruising satire, and his epistolary *cura*, as figures for the 'relaxation' that his demure show-villa affords and signifies (vv. 101ff.).[244] He winds up to a final vision of unclouded inspiration for prolonged active life: 'I pray you may break Nestor's world-record for living on' (v. 110, *finem Nestoreae precor egrediare senectae. //*). The prayer is fulfilled at once by suggestively 'exceeding this strong closure' to the poem. For it reverberates on through Gallicus' poem. The proverbial figure of Nestor is cued as the Pindaric figure, the Nestor we soon meet in the finale of 1. 4 (vv. 125ff.). As we think over Gallicus' poem, we will find that 'Nestor' pointed, not aside into cliché,[245] but ahead, all along, from the finale of the preceding poem to that of its chief mythic model, Pindar's *Third Pythian* (see Appendix).

Nestor's status as both the *Iliad*'s paradigm of wise counsellor to the Achaean King of kings, and the *Odyssey*'s survivor of all the tribulations that could overwhelm victorious heroes, will usher in another sequoia among evergreens (between the groom Stella and the 'boy' Etruscus of 1. 5. 64), Domitian's indispensable minister Gallicus, 'sixty years young' (v. 54). The effect works wondrously well, and (as if) by design.

Yes, the prayer for Vopiscus will cross over into the space of Gallicus' thanksgiving: the first three verses of 1. 4 would directly answer the prayer for Vopiscus, across any *paragraphos* or *coronis* that may have distinguished the ancient poems in their continuous columns.[246] Only when we run into the enjambed *Gallicus* (v. 4) will the new scenario disentangle in re-reading!

[2] Further depth emerges from superimposing Gallicus on Vopiscus. The 'cloudless breast' wished for rested Vopiscus (3. 109, *sic omni detertus pectora nube*) will gain point from, and bring point to, those unremitting labours of Gallicus as they crisis in his illness, 'infections, and coma's glowering cloudbanks of sick sleep' (vv. 109ff., *pestes / et suspecta mali . . . nubila somni*).

[3] The cadences of 1. 4. 7 and 52 will echo and re-echo 1. 3's last word, 'old age'—dangled over Gallicus (*senectae. /*). Continuation of this theme of *salus* also fulfils the final prayers for Stella's happiness ever after. For 1. 2 closed with the wish: 'May your looks last, may this beauty be slow to age', leaving its last word to resound through the book: *senescat. /*. Further pumping up the volume is the close of 1. 5, 'May what you have age with you, may your fortune learn better at once its renaissance' (*tecum ista senescant / et tua iam melius discat fortuna renasci*). The imperial prayer that ends 1. 1 got the sequence on the road: 'May you be blessed, may you see, offering incense to this offering, your—grandsons' (*laetus huic dono uideas dare tura nepotes*). And the concatenation of images of future generations reproduced and old age refreshed culminates in the imperial end to the book, 'so long as . . ., so long as Rome shall stand firm, your Rome, and so long as the Capitol you restore to the world shall endure' (. . . / *dum* . . . / *dum* stabit *tua Roma dumque terris / quod reddis Capitolium* manebit. /, 1. 6. 100–2).[247]

[4] Here the poet throws his book's lot in with Domitian's happy Christmases future, against any Roman decline and fall. The servant Gallicus will indeed have modelled for his emperor's salvation of Rome, we can now realise afresh, in retrospect: 'Stands right by your side, head unbowed' (v. 6, stat *proxima ceruix* . . .) . . . 'Still alive! Long as the aeon comes round again, he will live on!' (v. 15, *quippe manet longumque aeuo redeunte manebit*).

Statius will only come to include the rubric 'lyric' in the *Preface* to *Siluae* IV, and does not risk metrical virtuosity before that book, the second phase in his production of occasional poems.[248] But he displays his affiliation to Horatian lyric within the Virgilian climaxes to Book I's book-end imperial poems. Prayers end the first—saecular[249]—song proper in Horace's first collection of *Carmina* (after his stichic proem, 1. 1): 'On earth . . ., may you return late to heaven and long be happy in the company of your people . . ., here may you love being titled "Father"' (*Carm.* 1. 2. 42–50). These are amplified in those conspicuously confident prayers that end the first of the *Siluae*: 'May you be our lodestar, love the earth, may the palace of heaven hold no charm for you and—may you be happy to see your grandsons', 1. 1. 105–7).

Statius' same opening poem introduces these prayers for august Domitian with displayed elaboration of the famous *epilogue* to Horace's collection: 'I have crafted a memorial more lasting than bronze which no nibbling rain, no unruly wind could destroy, nor the row of years beyond count, nor the escape of time after time' (*Carm.* 3. 30. 1–5). He transfers the poet's Pindarizing claim to eternity for his work onto the imperial statue which forms both his own work of representation and the work that symbolizes the rei(g)ning Caesar: 'This work shivers at no rainy winters, nor the Almighty's triple flash, no legions from Aeolus' prison, nor the hold-ups of years: it will stand firm so long as . . ., so long as . . .' (1. 1. 91–4). Maybe he even reads 'through' Horace to his reference, Pind. *Pythian* 6, 'A treasure-house of hymns which neither wintry rain coming to invade, an army of thundering cloud without compassion, nor wind will smash' (8–13). His horse/poem stands for his monument: 'The horse stands firm', 84f., *equus . . . stat* ~ 'This work will stand firm', 91–3, *hoc . . . opus . . . stabit.*

Statius' finale to his book resumes this intertextual creativity. There he looks forward to an eternity for Domitian's re-creation of Rome in the revised calendar. The new Christmas ceremonies will be a holy day holiday to recur each and every year into infinity, to stand for imperial and poetic immortality, à la Horace: 'so long as the priest climbs the Capitol' (*Carm.* 3. 30. 8f.) ~ 'To think of the far-off years this day will pass through! This holy day will never vanish from whatever aeon! So long . . ., so long as Rome will stand firm, your Rome, and on earth the Capitol you restore will endure' (1. 6. 98–102).

The insertion of Rutilius Gallicus into Statius' Horatian web of imperial thanksgiving across the domain of the book-gathering is an important aspect of a reader's view of the minister's significance. The cue 'Horace' spells *for* 1. 4 not only celebration of Augustan society in a panorama of three inspired books,[250] and the poet-laureate's apogee as composer of the saecular song, but also the creator of the figure of the imperial servant through whose mediation duty to Rome is modelled for the élite, Maecenas. The prototype of deuteragony.

Gallicus will prove to be the one political heavyweight to take some of Domitian's limelight among the score of dedicatees who wander through the *Siluae* looking forward to maturity or the next siesta as *their* fitting *salus*.[251] Gallicus will stand out as Statius'

A ROMAN LIFE

paradigm of administrative *cura*, explored through its affinities to, and discontinuities from, the 'devotion to the state' of Horace's dedicatee. Statius' poet-and-prospective-minister dedicatee will read Gallicus through the poetic frame of Horace re-written.

At the same time, Statius and Gallicus claim for themselves and their emperor the mantle of Virgil and Capitoline Jupiter through evocation of the famous apostrophê of *Aeneid* IX: 'If my poetry has any power, no day will ever oust you from the aeon's memory, so long as the house of Aeneas shall dwell on the Capitol's bed-rock and the Father of Rome shall keep the Empire' (446–9). Whether we think of the 'happy pair' of poet and minister, poet and prince, or poet and poem, the point is, forever, the same: 'Lucky, both!' (446, *Fortunati ambo!*).

[5] Inclusion in the book shapes Gallicus' poem retrospectively as well as in prospect. Thus 1. 5, on the Baths of Claudius Etruscus, will supply the régime to complete the cure of 1. 4. Just what the doctor ordered! Both poems arrange for themselves cameo-excursions where the apparatus of Poesie—Apollo, Bacchus, Mercury, their Greek chorus-line—climb down (headily) from the heady heights of Mount Helicon's sublimity (vv. 19ff. ~ 5. 1–8).[252] Then the figurative wee 'spring' and 'rivulets' of poetic inspiration in 1. 4. 27f., 37 supply the elaborate artistry that the massively triumphant aqueducts feed all through 1. 5. In particular, 1. 5 re-considers the topic of *curae*, banishing the kind that make Rutilius Gallicus ill and the nation anxious along with its bard, and congratulating itself on the 'careful' investment of 'skill' its design manifests ('toil and nightwatch cares . . . What space could there be for my prayerful care among all these gatherings of the Roman people and their Fathers, the Senate?', vv. 54f., 115f., labor . . . *uigilesque . . .* curae, *quis mihi tot coetus inter populique patrumque / sit* curae uotique *locus ?* ~ 'Depart, the pair of you, Toil and Care! . . . Praise be, youngster, I pray, for your shining talent, for your care', 5. 11f., 63f., *discede*, Laborque / Curaque . . . *macte, oro, nitenti / ingenio* curaque *puer!*).

So exertions over Gallicus and his exertions earn a wallow in well-deserved relaxation, in Etruscus' newly customized *topos*. Both upwardly mobile, Rutilius *Gallicus* is to Claudius *Etruscus* as 'no pleb. soul' is to 'nothing pleb. *here*' (vv. 66f., *neque . . . plebeiam . . . animam* ~ 5. 47, *nil ibi plebeium est*).[253] In reading,

112

that is to say, 1. 4 'motivates' 1. 5, rather as Horace's first love(less) lyric *Ad Pyrrham* becomes *retroactively* an unanswerable argument in favour of the posture the poet next adopts in his rhetoric of *refusal* to fail stern Agrippa (in need, instead of Horace, of Varian epic).²⁵⁴ After Gallicus' gravity, Etruscus is light relief (1. 5. 9, 'I want to lower the tone for my gorgeous mate').

Finally, Statius' thoughts on Gallicus conclude in homiletic humilities: 'Ye gods have often . . . been won by turf and barley-meal, with just a shake of the salt-cellar' (vv. 130f.). This will dove-tail, or chime in, with the congenial dismissal of Poesie and Epic that guides 1. 5 down to its preferred start in Horatian sympotic levity. Here's the sort of fun denied poor Gallicus: the 'ladles to serve the toasts for the bath-warming party' *also* treat the reader-visitor to bath-house bathos with '¹/₁₂-pint-size (baby-) buckets for the staff to fill her up for the christening dip' (=1. 5. 10, *iunge, puer, cyathos*) !²⁵⁵

[6] Apollo rang Stella's wedding-bells (1. 2). He was *de trop* in the invocation for Gallicus—his own poet's poet (vv. 19–37). But not before time his mercy-dash saved the Prefect's day, and brought us *The Life of Gallicus*. Twin *apokeryxes* (dismissals) of Apollo that start 1. 5 and 1. 6²⁵⁶ will take the book out. Thus 1. 4 'mediates' between celebration and dismissal of Apollo, as Statius explores the range of modes his lyric hexameters can play—songs all the way from silly party-tunes to bursts of roaring epic, all in the same poetic wood, often up the same *Siluan* tree.

Preface signalled temporal transformation in the gathering of the separate folios into the set. What does this amount to? In brief, to the opening to reading of the composer's thinking, pre-thinking, and re-thinking. Safe in the environment of our book, we can relax from all the huffing and puffing of macho social-climbing political ambition, and the associated tilt against mortality.²⁵⁷ *Siluae* challenge us to respond to their 're-writing'. This may have been actual, virtual, or potential, and we may be certain, sure, suspicious, or prepared to suspend disbelief about it. Anyhow, traces of 'first thoughts' are on view in the poems, overlaid by such authorial 're-write'. The book-work of re-presentation is on show. The result is a proliferation of points of view, or polyphony of voices, radiating *from* the texts *through* the text. Six different ways to offer this new Virgil's new version of Horace. Pre-epic and post-epic, to one side of epic; elegy and epithalamium for Stella; satiric/epistolary *sermones* from the drawing-room of a Vopiscus . . .[258] Micro-wave lyrics played impromptu by the maestro on the scales of hexametric casualness.

'Let pygmies legitimately compare with giants' (5. 61f., *fas sit componere magnis / parua*).[259] Can Gallicus win the book for grandeur, a rebuke and hostage for the insidious seductions of cultured relaxation? Remember that Statius means us to think *Siluae* I over *Gallicus'* shoulder, too—as much an expert scribbler and critic as any of the other writers, one more Roman Apollo. Or will the overload of consular gravity bury the collection of precious insubstantiality under its long years of battling for Rome? Is *Siluae* I the best show in town, where you can watch encomium at work, see it gel, fail to gel? At no visible distance from the court, the poet laureate's 'off-cuts' are admirable not least for disclaiming our admiration (He *can* only let the emperor's majesty down . . .). 'Perhaps', as Statius puts it, elsewhere: 'I ready this offering for you on your birthday. It is miniscule, the poetic of miniaturism. *Who knows* if it won't live through the great aeons, the immortality of an epic?' (2. 3. 62: *forsan*). The *Siluae* turn on this risk-principle, and work through the predicament. At Domitian's service, and at ease, imperial courtiers must somehow build a viable lifestyle— enjoy every tasteful moment under the sword of Damocles. In their own time (*if* there could be such a thing). Their model, young Domitian, had been there himself, remember—poet, critic, devotee of Minerva, before the cares of state took away all his time on earth.[260]

In Gallicus' case, career inscription is re-presented as a bonus new lease of life; both were always projected to 'stand' in the necessary future as sepulchral epitaph, and 'live on', maybe, for as long as there should survive any *Roman Life*.

Ephemeral eternality.

Appendix

Thanks to Pindar:
Pythian 3

We have found *Siluae* 1. 4 working with Ovid's classic narrations of the myth of Coronis (chapter 15). Coronis was shot down on Apollo's orders for infidelity; their unborn child Asklepios was saved by its father from the pyre, and brought up in centaur Chiron's cave; here this junior leech learned medicine, but when he dabbled in resurrection (of Hippolytos/Virbius), an outraged bolt from the Almighty zapped him. In the sequel, Jupiter was obliged by Apollo to resurrect his grandson, and so violate his own veto. Statius has worked hints of Pindar into 1. 4 (vv. 27f., 37; and in the finale of 1. 3: chapter 20).[261] There is good reason to suppose that he expects a Stella, or a Vopiscus, to look through his effusion for Graeco-Roman synthesis, and find Pindar: one fresh-freed Dr *Pindarus*, for example, had cured Epicurean Cassius of the cares of life, by invitation; a second Dr *Pindarus* was boasted by Antonia Augusta's Roman household.[262] In what survives of Pindar, at any rate, '*Pythian* 3 puts unusual emphasis on two themes: human mortality and the power of poetry to transcend it'.[263] The third triad of this poem is launched by Apollo's dramatic 'fetching' of Asclepios to Chiron, to learn 'to heal a barrow-load of affliction: the diseases of mortals' (45f., ending the second epode). It is hard to believe this passage did *not* figure in the design of Gallicus' *soteria*.

Here is a translation of this central triad (47–69):

Those humans, now, all that came along with their self-sown   [strophe]
minders, their sores, or steel bayonet-wounded bodies,
or long-range missile casualties,
or summer fever's physical ravages or winter's, he released each
    one, guiding from their different
agues, treating some with soft spells,
others downing mild potions, or right around the limbs wrapping
    medications,
yet others he set back on their feet with the chop.

But even genius is hand-cuffed to graft.   [antistrophe]
Even he was swayed by a meaty fee, gold crossing his palms,
to fetch a man from death who was
already in custody. So the hand of Kronos' son lasered the breath
    rising up from both men's lungs,
mowed them down instantly, and blazing lightning leant deathstiny
    on them.
It must be that what befits mortal minds must be sought from the
    powers above,
no one overlooking what is in front of their feet, and recognizing
    our fraction of the scheme of things.

No! My own, my very self! Life without death, divinity—never   [epode]
chase it! Pump whatever actually works for all you're worth.
If sane Chiron still occupied his cave, and some sort of
love-drug put in his heart by the sweetness
of my singing, I would have swayed him to deliver some healer,
even in these days, to relieve good men of hot diseases
—some son of Leto's son (Apollo), say, or his father's (Father
    Zeus's) son—
then I should have come by ship chopping through the Ionian sea
to Arethusa's spring to join my guest-friend at Aetna,

who . . .

The strophe dances a whirl of injuries and their treatments; matching
antistrophe turns up the other side of the coin (as throughout this
unusual lyric),[264] acts out the failure of Asklepios' success story, until
the *choros* stops short, warned and warning us to behave as mortals
must; epode seizes this still moment of insight, climax to the myth, 'the

precise center of the ode's symmetry and . . . its central message in the simplest and strongest statement',[265] and makes it last, surging into the next triad, for not *all* human contriving is necessarily offensive. Short of raising the dead, it could be possible to wish without transgression to be cured of ills? The ode will explore further twisting and turning myths that may deplore / recuperate human gains and indemnities (double), before we arrive at Nestor paired with Sarpedon (survivor with war-dead). Their 'virtue's longevity' is down to 'fame in epic': Pindar's closural *gnome* (maxim) proclaims: 'For few is it easy to manage' (115).

The singer does not merely heroize the power of (his) song, which may often founder on the reef of praxis. No, this coda is as 'pharmacological' as Statius' was. Is it a parting barb? Vaunting that 'I, Pindar('s chorus), can deliver on this'?[266] Or flaunting obeisance to a sick Sicilian tyrant? 'How rare for a singer like myself to be handed the certainty of immortalization—as your hymnist.' Or is this (sane) euphemism? 'Don't bank on it.' Or flat denial, short of averring it? 'An impossibility for anyone! It just can't be done—and there's an end on't.' Or does this lyric stop . . . short of hybris . . . by sticking . . . at a maxim? 'Once in a millennium, one in a million, don't get your hopes up (too far)—It *can* be done, but before getting hopes up—let's draw the line under that! *Amen.*'

Now it is noticeable that the entire performance to this point has strung together a dominating series of seven 'if''s (2, 63, 73, 80, 86, 103, 110). Their grammar, syntax, rhetorical topicality and structural role are disputed. If I were to be right, each 'if' would oscillate between 'if (but no, it can never be . . .)', and 'if only (so may it prove . . .)'. We can try this out on 'if' at 63, but Pindar has already set out the dynamic of his lesson best in the opening strophe (1–7):

> I would/could wish for the son of Philyra [= Chiron],
> if I had to voice with my tongue what everyone says,
> that the one who has gone away should live,
> imperial child of Uranian Kronos, and over Pelion's glens held sway,
>   the wilderness beast
> with philanthropic intent—just as he was when once he raised
> the gentle craftsman of pain-relief through body, Asklepios
> the hero who keeps off the legions of disease.

This wish, if Pindar were to make it, and he is so far from this that he may only be reporting a (common-or-garden) wish, would be (would

117

want to be, wishes to be, would wish it were) a wish which is so far from speaking out perilously true commitment that not only are the name and circumstances of the object of concern withheld (Hieron of Syracuse), but even the name of the safely mythological creature who might discreetly mediate this wish all the way to life-saving intervention could not be further from the lips, and indeed thoughts, of this god-fearing people. This wish would be (the) one that the community would in a world of their choice want him to make. (Not that they come out and say so, and he would not himself even venture to voice the wish so that it could be heard, *unless* it might win approval. . .) All mortals will pass away, may be missed, might live on in some get-lucky memorialization. But to say so—really could put the lid on it.

Pindar's myth of Asklepios sets the pace for Statius' *soteria*, which finds ways of its own to negotiate the predicaments of prayers against inexorability, resorting to just three 'if's (vv. 31, 94, 128), and its own strategies to elude (counter-productive) assertion. Getting Apollo to summarize for his (un)fortunate son all the facts of Gallicus' *Life* provides 1. 4's most extensive and joyous circumvention of the fragilities of prayer.

Notes

[1] For some rivals neatly sketched, cf. McDermott and Orentzel (1979).

[2] See Norris (1987) 28–62.

[3] Shilts (1988) 476.

[4] On *Siluae* 1. 4: Hardie (1983) makes this 'Civil Service' poem his climax and culmination, 195–8, 'Silvae 1, 4. Rutilius Gallicus and the *novum saeculum*'; cf. 187–9, 'The *elogium* of Rutilius Gallicus: a model career'; cf. Vessey (1986) 2785–91 'The health of a prefect', Szelest (1971–2), Newmyer (1979) 93ff., Bright (1980) 56f.

On *Sittengeschichte*: Friedländer (1881) 451–6, reporting the unutterably elaborate disputations of the day (with successive input from Stobbe, Nohl, and Friedländer himself; cf. Friedländer (1870), (1880), etc.). See chapters 8, 14.

On the *soteria*: esp. Szelest (1968) and (1971–2) 435f., comparing a set of polished epigrams from the Greek Anthology and from Martial; cf. Cairns (1972) 73, 'This is the speech of rejoicing, congratulations and thanksgiving for the safety of someone who has been rescued from danger or has recovered from illness. . . . The *soteria*'s thanksgiving is addressed to a god, but . . . the man whose recovery or safety is being celebrated . . ., strictly speaking, is the addressee (object) of the speech. . . . The form of the generic title *soteria*, which refers properly to the sacrifices made in thanksgiving for recovery, is probably a sign of the importance of the subordinate religious element in the generic situation. The *soteria*, then, is a specialized form of eucharistic utterance'; cf. 154, 223f., in connection with Prop. 2. 28, Hor. *Carm.* 2. 17. Nisbet and Hubbard (1978) 272f. on Hor. *Carm.* 2. 17 set out the materials and conclude that 'Our poem should be seen in part as an original formulation of the *soteria*'. Cairns (1992) esp. 93 finds the acclamation of Maecenas' recovery in Hor. *Carm.* 1. 20 'parallel to the later illness and recovery of the *praefectus urbi*, C. Rutilius Gallicus, and the celebrations for it in AD 88'. These discussions follow Hardie's lead; Yardley (1977) queries generic bonding in the *soteria*. See esp. chapter 19.

On Gallicus as author: Duret (1986) 3244, 3271f. Cf. chapter 20.

On the *consilium*, Crook (1955) 181: no. 297, Jones (1992) 56.

On the Urban prefect, Vitucci (1956) 52, 69, Gsell (1967) 64f., 'Charactère du gouvernement de Domitien', cf. Syme (1988) 608–21, 'Prefects of the City, Vespasian to Trajan', esp. 615, Vigneaux (1896) 65f. See chapters 3, 6, 8, 9.

On Gallicus the priest, Lewis (1955) 136, *sodales Augustales* no. 25. See chapter 1.

On *Kaiserkult* here, Scott (1933) 249, 252f., 255 and (1975) 89, 114, 117, 134, 151; cf. Sauter (1934) esp. 24, 100, 115, 117. In revulsion, Chilver (1941) 100, 'Rutilius Gallicus was the sort of man whom Statius and Martial could praise'; contrast J. Wight Duff in *CAH* (1936) XI: 773f., with *Silv.* 1. 4. 130f. as climax to 'a ferment of noble conceptions in religion': 'good conscience . . . outweighing costly sacrifice'. See chapter 12.

On the *ludi saeculares*: Pighi (1965): 9, 79. See chapters 3, 4, 7, 12, 13, 15, 20.

On Asklepios: Weinreich (1908) 35, Scarborough (1969) 104. See chapter 15, Appendix.

On prosopography: Syme (1988) 517, cf. esp. Eck (1970) index s.v., esp. 57, 60, 123f.; for older bibliography cf. esp. Keil (1914) 194 n. 1. See chapters 1–4.

[5] Cf. During (1992) 50, 'Foucault argues that during the eighteenth century a "nosopolitics" emerges, whose sweep is larger than any more visible division between public and private medicine. Its object is the "social body"—that is, the population considered as a biological entity.' For plague 'as a kind of extended metaphor on the disintegration of the body politic', cf. Mittelstadt (1968) 148 (145 n. 1: inspired by Miss Wendy Schlesinger).

[6] Groag (1920) 1262.

[7] Syme (1991) 623.

[8] Braithwaite (1927) 52f. Groag (**1920**) 1255 did well to begin the *RE* entry on Gallicus by pointing up the importance of his *Ehreninschrift*, found at Ephesus in **1913** (only just in time to make Dessau's *Addenda* in Volume III, Part II, published in Berlin, **1916**), cf. 1256. 35ff., 'Erst Inschriftenfunde der jüngsten Zeit geben uns den authentischen Kommentar zur *laudatio*'.

[9] Desjardins (1877); (1877A) 192; cf. the more recent version in Jones (1979) 116f.: no. 250.

[10] Scott (1975) 151.

[11] Syme (1991) 629. This enthusiasm takes hold particularly once the reading of *illi quoque* in 1. 4. 71 as of Gallicus' grandfather, with *hunc* in 76 resuming focus on Gallicus with indenture for a new 'paragraph', seizes its author (esp. (1988) 517f., (1991) 628f.). M. G(riffin) (1990) proposes C. Rutilius Gallicus as avatar for Sir Ronald Syme: 1. 4. 52b, 54–6a head the obituary—but *suo pro Caesare curae* (v. 55) doesn't sound much like Syme? (v. 53 must be dropped because it would set a score of years distance between the brace of heroes).

For prosopographical discussion, cf. esp. Hardie (1983) 58ff., 68, Desjardins (1877), Groag (1920), Eck (1985), Syme (1988) 514–20, 'Statius on Rutilius Gallicus', (1991) 620–34, 'Turin's Two Senators', cf. 530.

[12] Cf. Salomies (1992) 116f., who resumés most of the inscriptions, Syme (1991) 627.

[13] Christol and Demougin (1985), Syme (1991) 629.

[14] Ritterling (1925) 1725, 1715. Cf. *ILS* 2288 for the end of Antoninus Pius' reign.

[15] Tac. *Hist.* 5. 1, *quinta et decima, uetus Vespasiani miles*, cf. Braithwaite (1927) 31f. on Suet. *Vesp.* 4. 6.

[16] Tac. *Hist.* 2. 79. They were pipped by another aide of Corbulo, the future right-hand man to Titus against Jerusalem and fabulously named Prefect of Egypt, *Tiberius Iulius Alexander*, who both poetically and tidily (i.e. memorably) took what became the official date for the Flavian plunge: 1 July 69 CE, Alexandria.

[17] Ritterling (1925) 1750f., 1755. So listed at the end of Antoninus Pius' reign (*ILS* 2288).

[18] Syme (1979–84) 42–6, 'Pamphylia from Augustus to Vespasian', solemnly 'corrects' Statius' misleading order here, waxing indignant with mortals' flawed geopolitical acumen. (Early thoughts account for J. G. C. Anderson's note in *CAH* (1934) X: 877, 'The Position held by Quirinius for the Homanadensian War', which relies on v. 77).

[19] *CAH* (1936) XI: 597.

[20] Tac. *Hist.* 2. 9 does have Galba put *Galatiam ac Pamphyliam prouincias* under a single commander.

[21] *ILS* 5025: replaced by Tettienus Serenus.

[22] Cf. Tac. *Hist.* 1. 77. 10, 2. 71. 8, 3. 55. 8, 4. 39, 4. 47; Dio 65. 2. 3. *FCIR* 223 has Gallicus' consulates among '*Nomi*' as '71 or 72; before 87'.

[23] 'Nero': Tac. *Hist.* 2. 6–9; Fonteius: ibid. 3. 46; Mucianus marched through Galatia to Byzantium, then across Thrace; Vespasian 'sailed to Lycia, then went by land and sea to Brundisium'. Lucky Asia was now virtually a demilitarized zone, though as strategically important for finance and supply-lines as it had been in triumviral days (Henderson (1994)).

[24] *ILS* 5955, where Gallicus helps settle provincial boundaries in Africa: gets his name on markers of 'the royal dyke'.

[25] For Gallicus as *legatus censitor*, cf. Thomasson (1982) 308, 312: no. 12. Part of the *census* of Vespasian and Titus, in 73/4, ibid. 318.

Grateful Leptis in Africa honoured Gallicus' wife, Minicia Paetina, with a statue in Turin, *ILS* 1008: the inscription found *Taurinis in moenibus*, 'in/on the walls of Turin'. Karen Henderson deserves one of these.

[26] For Domitian's provincial appointments, cf. Frezouls (1994).

[27] Buttrey (1975) esp. 29.

[28] Syme (1988) 516.

[29] Eck (1984) 149f.

[30] Hopkins (1991) 144.

[31] Cf. Woolf (1996), extending (e.g.) MacMullen (1982), Meyer (1990).

[32] See *PIR*[3] 1. 67, A. 393, *PME* 1. 84 A. 85, for what little is known of (the equestrian) Aemilius Pius.

[33] These walls were seventh-eighth century defences against Arab incursions, Foss (1979) 106. At Professor A. Bammer's request, Dr Helmut Engelmann in Vienna kindly checked for me that Keil's excavation *Skizzenbuch* (no. 1976) gives only what his *editio princeps* (1914) presents; and he found a 1992 record of the present location of the inscription at Ephesus. Joyce Reynolds kindly put me in touch with Dr Ulrike Outschar, who prevailed upon Dr Hans Taeuber of the Institut fur alte Geschichte, Altertumskunde

und Epigraphik, Universität Wien to locate, examine and photograph the stone: 'I found the stone right across the theatre, on the next parallel of the "Marmorstrasse" to the west, where it was obviously placed sometime after discovery. It had formed the central part of a basis which originally consisted of three pieces; the upper and lower parts are lost' (13 October 1997). I am greatly obliged to all these scholars, and especially to Dr Taeuber for his generous help and excellent photographs.

[34] Cf. MacMullen (1984). Birley (1982) 246 no. 12 lists Gallicus with other cases of military tribunate and legionary command (leg[atus] leg[ionis]) 'in the same army'.

[35] So Eck (1985), followed by Syme, e.g. (1991) 625. For Aemilius' cohorts, cf. Ritterling (1927) 30 (garrison in Asia), Eck (1972) 432 and n. 14 (attested in Galatia—under Corbulo).

[36] For 26, cf. Tac. Ann. 4. 55f.; for 40, cf. Dio 59. 28. 1: only the Pergamum cult of Rome and Augustus (after Actium), and Tiberius at Smyrna, lasted (not Gaius at Miletus); Domitian's temple was most likely retro-assigned to Vespasian. See Friesen (1993) esp. 7–28 (early Principate); 29–49 (Domitian=Price (1984) 255 no. 31)); 117–19 (Olympics). Ephesus was becoming a Roman city of marble, chock-a-block with lumps of empire: cf. Rogers (1991), esp. 1–38, 'The display of writing', 80–126, 'The procession of statues'. Vespasian 'even granted the Ephesians to celebrate some sacred games, a privilege he assigned to no other city.' (Dio 65. 9. 2: as a hypocritical boon to Balbillus the astrologer (PIR[1] 228, B. 41) . . .).

[37] Late antique Christian Ephesus smashed and defaced heaps of statues, erased miles of inscription (above all Artemis's), cf. Foss (1979) 32.

[38] Currie (1996) 83, 86 n. 16, on Odes 4. 4 and 15, crediting David West with the label 'epigraphic poetry'.

[39] Not to be missed, at v. 37, is displayed allusion to the 'Julian star' (Iulium sidus), via the Horatian echo of Carm. 1. 12.

[40] Catull. 11. 7, Serv. Aen. 10. 14, Maltby (1991) 25.

[41] Bendinelli (1929) 7.

[42] Martinelli (1978) 321, n. on 1. 4. 58 (But Syme (1991) 588 shows this is at least largely a compliment to Martial's addressee 'Domitius Apollinaris', so Apollo need not have dominated Vercellae. Turin was in Regio IX Liguria.) Promis (1869) 465, no. 223 offers the discredited scrap of evidence there is for Apollo in Turin itself (see Vollmer (1971) 289; there is no lore for the promising nearby 'Grecian Alps', Alpes Graiae). Scholars have traditionally turned to Caes. Bell. Gall. 6. 17. 2, Galli habent opinionem Apollinem morbos depellere, 'The Gauls believe Apollo drives away disease', and thought of the native cults of Belenos and Grannus (for which, cf. Krug (1985) 176f., Sobel (1990) 17, 53–6).

[43] See Tac. Hist. 2. 66: 'obliterated by the later disaster to an other', sister, Cisalpine 'city': 'This was curtains for Cremona, founded in the days of the Hannibalic assault on Italy, a bastion against any force coming down through the Alps, including Gauls interfering across the River Po' (ibid. 3. 34). This is part of the pyrotechnic history of the brash Legio XIV Gemina and its revolting Batavian auxiliaries, cf. Davis (1992) 29f., 43.)

[44] Cf. Plut. *Dom.* 5, Scott (1975) 92, MacDonald (1982) 13 n. 36. On the palace, Stat. *Silu.* 4. 2, Jones (1996) 124f.

[45] Cairns (1979) 68ff., Foulon (1983) 185ff. on Tibullus 2. 5.

[46] Cf. Hor. *Carm.* 1. 32, with Nisbet and Hubbard (1970) *ad loc.*, Prop. 2. 31, with Hubbard (1984) 289f., cf. Fishwick (1987) 81f., Zanker (1988) *passim.* Hor. *Epp.* 1. 3. 17 first speaks aloud the scholarly resources of *Palatinus* Apollo.

[47] Cf. Cairns (1984) 153 on Prop. 4. 6.

[48] Keppie (1983) 16–8, cf. 205, 'Augusta Taurinorum (Turin)', 'The precise date of foundation cannot be established', ibid. n. 120, 'Chilver [(1941) 20f.] preferred to see Turin as a civilian colony founded in 27 BC.' For a recent survey cf. Culasso Gastaldi (1988).

[49] Cf. Bendinelli (1929) Tav. XIV, Fig. 17, 'Pianta di Torino nel 1416'.

[50] Zanker (1988) 329, caption for Figure 4. Studies by Kähler (1942) 58f., 101f., Richmond (1943); cf. Cavaliere Manasse, Massari, Rossignani (1982) 43–52, 'Torino e la Valle di Susa', esp. 48f. (a reference I owe to John Patterson.)

[51] Cf. ibid. 4, 'for healing the illness and easing the sickness there was no divine or human resource which Titus did not bring to bear. He had research done into every kind of sacrifice and remedy.'

[52] We find Domitian building a new temple on the Capitol, to '*Iuppiter Custos*' ('Jove the Warden', Suet. *Dom.* 5).

[53] Cf. Bendinelli (1929) 46, Pascal (1964) 36 and n. 2.

[54] Desjardins (1877) 30; cf. Robinson (1992) 183, 187–91, Carter (1982) 149 on Suet. *Aug.* 37. 1, for accounts of this magistracy.

[55] Millar (1977) 312; Hardie (1983) 187.

[56] DuQuesnay (1984) 26, cf. Cairns (1992) 92f., '31–29 BC, . . . the time when Maecenas was . . . *de facto* what was later called *praefectus urbi*; and indeed some sources anachronistically refer to him in language normally used of a *praefectus*'. Reinhold (1988) 40f. on Dio 49. 16. 2 explains that 'Though Maecenas had wide-ranging authority, with police power, in Rome and the rest of Italy, he did not of course have the title *praefectus urbi*; his role was, in fact, closer to that of the later *praefectus praetorio*.'

[57] Nisbet and Hubbard (1970) 80, Introduction to *Carm.* 1. 6, cf. 83, 'the grim general', 84, 'the fieldmarshal', etc.; Zanker (1988) 71; Reinhold (1988) 26 on Dio 49. 4. 1–4; cf. Woodman (1983) 198f. on Vell. 2. 79. 1.

[58] Cf. Suet. *Dom.* 4. 3.

[59] Vessey (1986) 2791; Newmyer (1979) 94 n. 31.

[60] In the satirist's catachresis, *uilicus Vrbi* (*Sat.* 4. 77); cf. Syme (1991) 626: Suetonius abusively calls Domitian's Prefect of the City Arrecinus Clemens, freshly appointed in, and deceased soon after, 83, 'one of his intimates and special agents' (*Dom.* 11. 1).

[61] Syme (1991) 627; cf. Vigneaux (1896) 3 for later instances.

[62] Murison (1992) 154, 166, 168, 170.

[63] Vessey (1986) 2787, 'By irony, the antithetic figure of Sejanus lurks half-seen'.

[64] Martin and Woodman (1989) 194f., *ad loc.*, cf. Woodman (1977) 245–63 on

Vell. 2. 127f. So Augustus wrote to, and of, Tiberius, *unus homo nobis uigilando restituit rem* (Suet. *Tib.* 21. 5).

[65] Syme (1988) 620; cf. 'Next Statilius Taurus, however far over the hill, bore up magnificently . . .!' (Tac. *Ann.* 6. 11).

[66] Tac. *Ann* 12. 42. 2, 13. 2. 1, 14. 5. For Burrus's career, cf. McDermott (1949). These stereotypes are never descriptions, they are always partisan: 'He was called the Nazi Nero . . . Goebbels called him "the upright soldier with a child's heart." Konrad Heiden . . . added ". . . and with a child's brain." The American ambassador . . . saw in him "a fat, ridiculous-looking man." . . . Sir Nevile Henderson found "certain attractive qualities" in him and added: "I must frankly say that I had a real personal liking for him." . . . To some of his friends he was "the last real Renaissance figure." I have heard him described as "the modern version of a Roman pro-Consul." He liked to think of himself as a "German Maecenas." His enemies reply that he was "the greatest thief of contemporary history". He has been called a Falstaff, a buccaneer, a hero, a playboy, a great diplomat, a ruthless adventurer, a likeable bully, an able administrator, a cunning politician, simple, vain, brutal, at the same time.' (Frischauer (1960) *Preface*, 6, cf. 256, 'Goering was dead. He looked peaceful, with a sardonic smile around his lips.')

[67] On (*domi <> militiae*), cf. Richardson (1991) 7f.

[68] Hor. *Epp.* 1. 5. 4, *iterum Tauro*. For the record, 'The wine can be at the most six years old, and is of undistinguished origin, but has a pleasant connotation' (Kilpatrick (1986) 63, 140 n. 46). 'Taurus' fits Horace's invitee, 'Torquatus' (3), both in sound and in (unpleasantly) hard-man connotation (through the proverbial link with the eponymous family-lore of *T. Manlius Imperiosus Torquatus*, cf. *imperium*, 6, with ibid. 62f.).

[69] *Serm.* 2. 6. 38, *Epod.* 9. 37, *Carm.* 3. 8. 17, 29, 24f., and—the last word—4. 11. 36.

[70] Henderson (1990) 185; Syme (1958) 790, cf. 560. Annius Vinicianus, the executed conspirator against Nero in 66, also married a daughter of Corbulo.

[71] Syme (1991) 624. Vidman (1982) 292–4, 302, argues for the order Plotius Pegasus—Fuluus—Gallicus—Arrecinus Clemens—Glitius Agricola.

[72] Syme (1991) 629f.—or Glitius may have struggled to get out of Gallicus' light, ibid. 601; cf. Alföldy (1982) 315, 359f.

[73] Syme (1991) 560, 626, Jones (1996) 98f. on Suet. *Dom.* 11. 1. Ibid. 8. 2, Domitian is specifically *credited* with *fine urban appointments*—in the main turning back to his father's supporters from the *coup* (Jones (1979) 17f.).

[74] German proverb.

[75] R. Syme in *CAH* (1936) XI: 172, followed closely *passim* by Jones (1992); cf. Southern (1997) 92–100.

[76] Henderson (1927) 163.

[77] Crook (1955) 52; maternal uncle of Titus' daughter Julia; Syme (1988) 516, (1991) 626.

[78] Cf. Suet. *Dom.* 4. 3, with Jones (1996) 41, cf. (1992) 203f., accepting Syme's reckoning that Domitian heeded an Augustan intention to change *saecula* in 23 BCE, before postponement to 17 BCE.

[79] Although Domitian took the consulate for 90, he then missed 91, 93, 94, 96, so 89 proves to have introduced a policy from which he was not deflected. The thirteen *coss.* of 90 would line up a striking parade of loyalty rewarded, and confidence in the reign—if the effort did not betray anxiety, and fear (cf. Hardie (1983) 189).

[80] See Syme (1979–84) 1070–84, 'Antonius Saturninus', esp. 1081 for refusal to judge Antonius' aims: conceivably he did declare himself the new Caesar. Court-speak had dubbed each new inauguration of a Domitianic consular year the start of a new *saeculum*, cf. Coleman (1988) 72f. on *Silu.* 4. 1. 17–18. Consuls could still seem possible challengers for the purple, cf. Suet. *Dom.* 10. 4, where Flavius Sabinus (grandson of Vespasian's brother Sabinus) was eliminated because the election-day herald had boobed and declared Sabinus 'not consul but emperor'. As Jones (1992) 147 avers, Saturninus will have been mindful of the two legions' proclamation of Vitellius at Mainz on 1 January 69 (an unhappy precedent.)

[81] R. Syme in *CAH* (1936) XI: 173 (following the re-construction of E. Ritterling); cf. Southern (1997) 101f.

[82] So Mart. 4. 11, where 'Saturninus', aptly nicknamed to be a carnival Aunt Sally, is 'distended by his name', both because *Antonii* did not normally boast *cognomina* and by a pun on *satur*, 'full (of food)'; he 'stirred up civil war under the North Pole', 3, as mirror-image of Antony and Cleopatra in the deep south; he should have remembered the 'Deathstiny' of his *nomen*, sunk in the Actian's sea, not hoped that Rhine's 'Arctoan waters' would do for him what Nile had failed to do for Mark Antony (5–8): cf. 'Arctoan hordes and the Rhine in uprising' (v. 89).

[83] R. Syme in *CAH* (1936) XI: 176.

[84] History would compel a look back to 69 and Otho's partially successful · attempt to keep Vitellius' German mutiny/invasion of Italy blocked at the Alps by a lightning landing of urban cohorts, praetorians and marines from the fleet (cf. Murison (1992) 115f.).

[85] For Domitian's staggered but committed assumption of the triumphal *agnomen* 'Germanicus', cf. Southern (1997) 81f. Along with *Domitianus*, the name was religiously erased from monuments after his 'damnation of memory', presumably because it was specially honorific, not just a routine title (cf. Merkelbach (1979)).

[86] Cf. 'When at the very deadline for the decisive confrontation a sudden melt-down of the Rhine reined in the alien forces poised to cross and join Antonius', Suet. *Dom.* 6. 2 (on Saturninus' revolt).

[87] Suet. *Dom.* 15. 1, cf. Hardie (1983) 189f.

[88] 'Evidence converges to disclose a pestilence and a whole run of unhealthy years . . ., a plethora of deaths, carrying off both the young and the mature', Syme (1991) 593, cf. ibid. 564.

[89] Most (1990) 132.

[90] Thus Fry (1980) persuasively locates 'the poet's calling' in the entwined senses of that phrase.

[91] *Cura* had military application, as well as political, hegemonic, titular, medical, emotional, etc. (Cf. Woodman (1977) 145 on Vell. 2. 106. 3).

[92] Cairns (1992) 93, referring to Hardie (1983) 197.

[93] Beard (1991) explains how 'writing and ancient paganism' are 'inextricably intertwined: there will be no understanding of Graeco-Roman paganism without an understanding of its textual strategies' (58).

[94] Syme (1958) 97, the sentence which this book pretty well glosses.

[95] Statius' asseveration already cues emperor cult, as in 'Sure salvation of the world, glory of the earth, Caesar, through whose safety we believe there are gods' (Mart. 2. 91. 1f., *Rerum certa salus, terrarum gloria, Caesar, / sospite quo magnos credimus esse deos //*). But both Propertius' 'The Dead *are* something' (4. 7. 1, *Sunt aliquid manes*) and Ovid's 'There *are* gods—go on, believe it' (*Am.* 3. 3. 1, *Esse deos, i, crede*, with its gloss, 'It pays off that there are gods and, as it pays off, let's suppose there are', *Ars* 1. 637, *expedit esse deos et, ut expedit, esse putemus*) provide diversionary literary interference; their matrix is Laertes' recognition of his son's return as if from the dead, exclaimed as Father recovered from his black-out after Odysseus' proof of identity: 'Father Zeus, YEA VERILY, you gods *are* there still on high Olympus, if the suitors truly have paid for their sinful violence . . .' (Hom. *Od.* 24. 351f., *Zeu pater, ê ra et' este theoi . . .*).

[96] See Petrey (1990) 161 for these points.

[97] Cf. Hor. *Carm.* 4. 2 for this written out to make a whole poem, which culminates, like *Silu.* 1. 4, in the contrast between grand bull-sacrifice in state and the poet's humble 'widow's mite': 'You will sing Caesar with your weighty plectrum ~ thrice "O Triumph!", more than once we shall cry "O Triumph!", the whole citizen-body, and we shall offer the kind gods incense. Ten bulls and 10 cows your price; mine shall be a tender calf' (1–52). On 'the topos of the 'poor offering of the humble donor", as in the celebration of Maecenas' recovery from illness of Hor. *Carm.* 1. 20, cf. Cairns (1992) 87 and n. 15, and chapter 18.

[98] For Clotho, cf. Stat. *Theb.* 3. 556, Ov. *Fast.* 6. 757, Sen. *Apocol.* 3. Stark *uoluo*, which suits epic unrolling of the *uolumen* of Fate (e.g. Virg. *Aen.* 1. 262), seems agreeably ponderous of spinning (Cf. Hor. *Carm.* 4. 2. 11, the torrential *force de nature* of lawless Pindaric lyric *uerba deuoluit*—taken up by Gray as 'the rich stream of music . . . / Now rolling down the steep amain, / Headlong, impetuous, see it pour' (cf. Jacobus (1985) 168 n. 4 on Cowley's *Pindarique Odes*); but cf. *fusis mollia pensa / deuoluunt*, 'they spin the soft wools off the distaffs', Virg. *Georg.* 4. 348f.). *Opus* is, though grandiose for a single life-thread (e.g. Catull. 64. 315), plainly at home of 'woman's work', the *pensum*.

There will turn out to have been an 'enallage' (rhetorical exchange) between the registers of imagery distributed between the opening and closing elements of the proem's ring-structure, vv. 1–18, with *Clotho . . . spoliare . . . exuit*, 'Spinner, stripping, taking off', 1, 5, 8 ~ *induerint*, 'put on', 17; *uoluit . . . fila*, 'rolls threads', 2, 7 ~ *fatis*, 'destiny', 17; *alma*, 'motherly', 2 ~ *mitis*, 'mild', 16; *pios*, 'godfearing', 2 ~ *peccauerit*, 'sinned', 18; *redit . . . reuirescit in annos*, 'returns, grows strong again for the years ahead', 3, 8 ~ *aeuo redeunte . . . instaurati*, 'as the aeon returns, renewed', 15, 18; *dubitata*, 'put in doubt', 3 ~ *intrepidae*, 'unafraid', 16; *sidera cernit /*, 3 ~ *saecula crimen /*,

17; *erubuit*, 'blushed', 5 ~ *crimen*, 'charge', 17; cf. *tanto*, 'so great', 5 ~ *tantum*, 'so great', 17; *stat*, 'stands firm', 6 ~ *manet . . . manebitque*, 'endures, shall endure', 15. Thickening this is the contra-flow between the poet's Neapolitan Hellenism at the onset and the emphatic reverberations of Romanness when he is joined by his massed congregation, *Clotho . . . Astraea*, 1–2 ~ *Romae . . . Tarenti*, 16–18 (cf. Newmyer (1979) 94 for this ring-structure.)

[99] Ovid. *Met.* 1. 150, *terras Astraea reliquit*, the start (we should reflect) of 'another' epic. The 'Saturnian' honeymoon period ushering in a new reign encouraged the same thought, cf. Philo *Leg. ad Gaium* 13.

[100] *-iliata redit,* ‖ *. . . -itataque . . . cernit* / has a convincing lilt to it, too.

[101] 'Stars' in Latin are inherently 'stable', cf. Serv. *ad Verg. Aen.* 5. 42, *stellae ab stando* (Maltby (1991) 582).

[102] Cf. Sauter (1934) 24ff., 'Der Kaiser als der Liebling der Götter und Menschen, *cura deorum*'.

[103] As if, moreover, in a chiasmus: *Gallicus es caelo ~ dis es Germanice*, hinged at the heterodyne central spondee: *-lo dís*, and framed by the emphatically anaphoric spondees: *és cael- ~ és Germ-* . Marastoni (1958) 25 applauds the metrical, rhythmic expressivity of this 'solida struttura'—but prints as 'due interrogazioni' with a '?' Further, sonic bonding of the line and its twin heroes, twin concepts of divinity and twin asseverations is provided by the pattern: *caelo* ‖ *dis ~ cordi* /.

[104] For this jargon in imperial service, cf. 'by so bravely taking the strain on your neck', Vell. 2. 131. 2, with Woodman (1977) 282 *ad loc.*

[105] Mortals make poor snakes: but *senectae* / *exuit*, vv. 6f., images (Aesculapian/heroic) renewal of life by 'sloughing'; cf. Ov. *Met.* 9. 266–8, 'as when a new snake takes off old age along with age . . ., so when Hercules stripped off mortal limbs' (*. . . senecta* / *. . . mortales . . . exuit artus* /), Cornutus *Theol. Gr.* 33 (explaining the Asklepian serpent), 'rejuvenating from illness, shedding his slough' (*ananeazon ek ton noson kai ekduesthai to gêras*), Macrob. 1. 20. 2, Knox (1950).

[106] Cf. and contrast (e.g.) Virg. *Ecl.* 10. 3, Ov. *Met.* 6. 193, etc.

[107] Cf. Vitucci (1956) 52, 69 for the envisaged encroachment on the praetorian preserves by 'trouble-shooter' City prefects. 'As commandant of the cohortes urbanae, the *praefectus urbi* was also responsible for public order in the capital and, from the second century on, up to 100 miles outside the city limits, beyond which (in Italy) the *praefectus praetorio* was operative' (Reinhold (1988) 191 on Dio 52. 21. 1–2, cf. Robinson (1992) 190).

[108] The matching of the second and final verses of the tricolon is particularly ornate: tu*um* ~ tua; *fora* tur*bida* ~ *implorant i*ura; que*stum* / ~ que*relis* /. The movement from the life of the city, military and civilian, out to the far-flung reaches of the peninsula, develops from the close-by alacrity of the guards' reverence through the dash to safety from the racket of the market-place, out to the distress signals beamed up from the Roman margins. *Longinquis*, 12, will at once bind space to time in its proximate reflex, *longum*, 15.

[109] / *certent . . . coll*is / con*fremat*, 13f., recaptures the echoes of col*unt . . . cohortes,* / *. . .* / con*fugiunt*, 9–11. or*dine . . . peioris* mur*mura* fa*mae* /, 13f.,

reverberates after ur*bana cohortes* . . . fora tur*bida* . . . con*fugiunt* . . . ur*besque* ubi*cumque togat*ae / . . . *implorant i*ura, 9–12. To sum up, *colunt* . . . *leges*, 9–11, and l*onginqui*s *implorant* . . . *quere*lis, 12, re-cycle in l*aetitia* . . . *c*ollis, 13, before re-versing into sil*eant*, 14. These affective 'Hills' of Rome echo in acclamation of the recovery from illness of the second citizen (Maecenas), in 'Mt. Vatican to deliver your bravo's, then the echo to deliver them back again' (Hor. *Carm.* 1. 20. 7, *redderet laudes tibi Vaticani / montis imago*, where Cairns (1992) esp. 97f., hears the aural likeness '*Vati-canus*' as **uates + cano*, 'Song of the Poet'. The poem's last word echoes on, and on: *colles. //* ('hills'), in a poem made of such SFX (esp. 5–11, paterni /, . . . Vaticani /, . . . Fa*lern*ae /, . . . Formiani /, and the final flourish, 10ff., *bibes* . . . *uites* . . . *pocula* colles. *//*). Philip Hardie hears Statian echoes of the landscape voicing celebration of Roman origins before time, Virg. *Ecl.* 5. 62ff., *ipsi* laetitia *uoces ad sidera iactant / intonsi montes* . . ., chiming with the saecular shock of cosmic joy in *Ecl.* 4. 52, *aspice, uenturo* laetantur *ut omnia saeclo*.

[110] Doubts over the text at v. 13 risk destroying the poem's mytho-logic which patterns, in traditional Latin fashion, *Italia* upon *Roma*. Yet it is not unfitting that the text should shatter just here, into the unintelligible unmistakability of its Roman roar of joy. Suet. *Dom.* 4. 5 reports a souped up *sacrum Septimontiale*. Mart. 8. 36. 5f. may date this to 93, or just before (cf. Richardson (1992) 349, Jones (1996) 48).

[111] Cf. Reinhold (1988) 191, 'An office to be held by a consular senator for life', Woodman (1977) 114 on Vell. 2. 98. 1: 'Piso, who held office for 20 years until his death in AD 32 . . ., became almost the archetypal Urban Prefect'.

For the proportionality: 'Prefect : Emperor :: Rome : Empire', cf. Woodman (1977) 136 on Vell. 2. 104. 2, the emperor as *custodem* . . . *imperii sui*.

[112] 1. 1. 54, cf. 'forever . . . forever . . . he shall stand firm' (ibid. 55, 99, 93: *stabit*); 1. 6. 101f., *stabit* . . . *manebit. /*. For Statius' repetition, cf. 'Those your statues . . . *endure and shall endure* as long as the very temple' (Plin. *Pan.* 52: *manent manebuntque*; Wills (1996) 302f. traces this hexameter-cadence idiom to Verg. *Aen.* 6. 617, *sedet aeternumque sedebit /*). For the verb, cf. 'While . . . while . . . while the rocks of the father shall stand firm, while . . . while . . . while the sublime grace of the Flavian clan *shall endure*' (Mart. 9. 1: *manebit*).

[113] *redit et uirgo, redeunt Saturnia regna* (with DuQuesnay (1976) 40ff. on the the 'Messianic' *Eclogue* as saecular); cf. 'Scorned Virtue dares return' (Hor. *Carm. Saec.* 58: *redire*).

[114] From 'mild rider' on (1. 1. 15, cf. 25, 102). Of the public servant's emollience, cf. 'if a juror's hostility needs placating, he'll manage to find mildness through your oratory' (*Paneg. Mess.* 46f.: *mitescere*).

[115] Putnam (1986) 19. *mitis* is also the axis of Aesculapian worship, cf. 'mild god' (3. 4. 25), 'mild Asklepios' (Pind. *Pyth.* 3. 6). And *mitis* will recur in 'mild fosterling' (v. 21).

[116] Cf. Sauter (1934) 4ff., 'I. Der Kaiser als *Soter*', esp. the cheers on Maecenas' return to the limelight after illness, Hor. *Carm.* 2. 17. 25f.

[117] The story starts: 'When the city and fields were wasted by a mighty pestilence, Valesius, once his sons and daughter were struggling so badly the doctors gave no hope . . .' (Val. Max. 2. 4. 5); or: '[*Saecula*] help with healing plagues, pandemics, diseases . . .: when a disease struck Valesius' children, beyond the reach of the doctors' art . . .; and in later times when a plague befell the city in the first year after the Kings, P. Valerius Publicola . . .; after that, when diseases and wars struck in 502 A. U. C. . . .; again during the onset of various desperations, Octavian Augustus renewed the festival . . .' (Zosimus 2. 1. 1ff.; cf. Pighi (1965) 47ff., Brind'Amour (1978)).

[118] Pighi (1965) 346, *incolumitatem sempiternam, uictoriam, ualetudinem populi Romani*. In the only complete text of a *carmen saeculare* we have, cf. the specification 'Phoebus who with the saving art relieves the body's worn limbs, if he looks fair upon the Palatine altar' (Hor. *Carm. Saec.* 63ff. For the remains of the Septimian song, see Pighi (1965) 224–7).

[119] For dread of the end of a *saeculum*, cf. DuQuesnay (1976) 41. On the crisis, cf. Hardie (1983) 195.

[120] This suggestion from Michael Reeve. D'Ambra (1993) 41 summarizes what (little) is known of Domitian's saecular games. Coins tell the sequence through, cf. *BMCRE* (1930) 2. xcvi: you need not expect Domitian to share his coins, but would he turn down the chance to ape Augustus ceremonially, for lack of an adequate deputy?

[121] See Poe (1984) esp. 64f.

[122] On the '*T*^{a}/$_e$*rentine*' aetiologies, see Pighi (1965) 33ff., Fishwick (1987) 88 and n. 36, Richardson (1992) 377.

[123] For the conceit, cf. Virg. *Georg.* 3. 42, 'My mind attempts nothing exalted/deep without you' (*te sine nil*), with White (1993) 20, 279 n. 39.

[124] 'So great a servant grows strong again', so now let him 'serve new strength and spirit' (*tanto . . . ministro / . . . reuirescit*, vv. 5, 8 ~ *uires . . . animumque ministra* /, v. 22, where Philip Hardie observes the figuration of poet as emperor, as well as the spark of divine paradox echoed from Virg. *Aen.* 5. 640, *deus ipse fac*es animumque ministra*t* /).

[125] With 'Don't you scorn worship from a lighter lyre' (vv. 34–6), cf. 'Don't spit out humble gifts' (*Paneg. Mess.* 7f.: in the proem).

[126] For *Aonian* Thebes, cf. Dewar (1991) 57f. on *Theb.* 9. 1; for Minerva and Domitian, cf. D'Ambra (1993) 10f. and *passim*.

[127] Statius is 'quoting' himself in/from *Theb.* 7. 5, *uelocem* || *Tegees . . . alumnum* /; for *Dircaean* Thebes, cf. Dewar (1991) 185 on *Theb.* 9. 679.

[128] A *centum*viral block-vote of confidence in their inspirational Marshal more than satisfies the poet's traditional longing for 'a hundred mouths with another hundred tongues' to do justice to a heroic theme! (Virgil's Sibyl, *Aen.* 6. 625f.). This was *the* prestige court of imperial Rome (Plin. *Epp.* 9. 23).

[129] Cf. 'without him' ~ 'without his divine favour' (vv. 19, 23, *sine illo* ~ *sine numine*), alluding to the epic cadence 'without the favour of the gods': *sine numine diuum* after *(ouk) aekêti theôn*.

[130] Cf. Callim. *Hymn to Apollo* 2. 108ff., 'Grand is the flow of the Assyrian river . . ., the drops from a holy spring are small', Wimmel (1960) esp. 230 n. 1. With mihi *gurges* in *haustos* /, v. 27, cf. tibi *dulcis* in *artem* /, v. 29. Statius

may re-work Hor. *Epp.* 1. 3. 10 here: [*Iulius* Florus] *Pindarici* font*is qui non expalluit* haustus /.

[131] Cf. Duret (1986) 3272 on the broad sweep of *facundia* here. Lyric Statius maybe unpacks Horace into his own free-wheeling conceit, cf. Hor. *Carm.* 4. 2. 10ff., *seu . . . numerisque fertur* / lege solutis //, *seu . . . siue . . .* ('whether Pindar dashes with metres set free from rules, or . . . or . . . or . . .'), the contained close of a Sapphic stanza set to describe the uncontainable energies of Pindaric dithyrambics. (Most (1990) 15 and n. 32 argues that *lege solutis* (falsely) alleges non-responsive meters; ibid. 14 n. 26 suggests that *Silu.* 5. 3. 151f., on the Teachings of Statius' Father, is implicit polemic against Horace's polemical description of Pindaric practice.)

[132] Ceres and Bacchus (bread and wine) form a pair; Diana and *Bellipotens* share hunt/battle (Statius thinks here of Nisus' prayer to Diana in Virg. *Aen.* 9. 404ff., '. . . any offerings my father fetched to your altar, any I added or hung up in your rotunda': *tu, dea, tu, . . .* / *astrorum decus . . .* / *si qua tuis . . . pater . . . aris* / *dona tulit, si qua . . . auxi* / *suspendiue tholo . . .*).

[133] For the formula *tu . . ., namque potes omnia*, cf. Virg. *Aen.* 6. 117, Callim. *Hymn.* 4. 226.

[134] Callim. *Hymn to Apollo* 2. 106, *oud' hosa pontos . . .*: Ocean (and Homer) were canonically hymned as 'the *source* of all rivers, all sea, all springs and wells' (*Il.* 22. 196f., see Williams (1978) 87–9 on Callim. *Hymn* 2. 105). *maius* /, v. 34, responds with *minores.* /, v. 37.

[135] Lühr (1880) 13 compared *quantum praecedit clara* minores / luna *faces* (*Silu.* 2. 6. 35f., 'as much as bright *moon* outstrips / the *lesser* torches'), but somehow missed 1. 4.

[136] Cf. Henderson (1997) 97–114. *Satirical* Horace had mocked just this sort of servile cringing (*Serm.* 1. 7. 23f., cf. Henderson (1994) 159). Domitian built a great temple to *Iuppiter Custos* (cf. Southern (1997) 140 n. 10).

[137] Cf. Wilson (1993) 233f. *cingitur*, 'is girt', befits soldierly Gallicus (v. 36, cf. vv. 75, 107).

[138] Callim. *Hymn to Apollo* 2 *ad fin.*, teaching Rome to read poetry *as* hymn to poetry.

[139] Mimetic 'historic presents' stud the basic structure of perfect tenses (vv. 49f., 60–2, 106–8, 110f.).

[140] On the difficult twist of lyric writing in v. 49, cf. Pitcher (1990) 92.

[141] Plut. *Num.* 22. 6; 21. 4, citing Calpurnius Piso; 21. 1.

[142] Plut. *Pomp.* 57. 1: the 'vows for the good health' of Pompey became an imperial precedent, cf. Fishwick (1987) 90 n. 48. Cic. *Tusc.* 1. 86 spread the moral (cf. Mayor (1886) 151f. on Juv. 10. 283.) Lucan links the thought to Pompey's night before Pharsalus: 'for you . . . the mob of women would have slashed their breasts, hair a riot, as at the death of Brutus' (7. 37–9: . . . femin*eum ceu* Bruti *funere uolgus*). Triumphs: ibid. 7. 19, *adhuc Romanus eques*; Horace: Peter Wiseman incisively reminds us of *Ars Poetica* 342, *celsi . . . Ramnes*, 'where the context makes them part of the theatre audience (cf. v. 113)'.

[143] Mourned by the *matronae* for a year and a day, Liv. 2. 7. 4.

[144] Cf. Robinson (1992) 187–91, Griffin (1976) 270, Gsell (1967) 65 on the duties envisaged here.

[145] Billeted along with the praetorians since Tiberius, Watson (1969) 18f.).

[146] / parcere *uerberibus* ('v. 44, spare the whips') must echo the climax of Anchises' definition of the Roman mission, / parcere *subiectis* . . . (Virg. *Aen.* 6. 853, 'spare the subdued'); Vessey (1986) 2787 also recognizes this 'recall'—an *hapax* in this *sedes*: / parcere). In: audire catenas, / . . . uerber*ibus* . . . ferr*um* (vv. 42–8, 'audible chains; whips; steel') hear Rhadamanthys' Tartarean tortures: *exaudiri gemitus et saeua sonare* / uerbera, *tum stridor* ferri *tractaeque* catenae / . . . (*Aen.* 6. 557f., 'far audible groans and the noise of raw whips, next the hiss of steel and the dragging of chains'. *catenae* only at Aen. 6. 558, 8. 225 in all Virgil. For uerba precant*um*, 'prayers' words', v. 46, cf. uerba precant*ia*, 'praying words', *Aen.* 7. 237.)

[147] So: 'I am famous as the one who, all too often, has managed to soften the pain of bereavement' (5. 5. 38f., *ille ego qui (quotiens!)* . . . *uiduos potui* mulcere *dolores*, cf. Gossage (1972) 213).

[148] Statius here profits from hexameter decorum and necessity to turn prosaic 'sixty years of age' into 'twice six *lustra*', as if heroes must be living 'quinquennial' religious festivals. *Orsa* inserts the image-repertoire of Clotho's 'spinning'.

[149] Cf. Metellus' challenge: 'an army slothful and unfit for war, in shape for neither crisis nor effort; the stains of laziness and luxuriousness' (Sall. *Bell. Iug.* 44. 1, 5). Corbulo would never stand for it: legions 'lazy through prolonged peace' (Tac. *Ann.* 13. 35, *pace longa segnes*). From the manual: Claud. *Paneg. IV cos Hon.* 8. 322ff., 'The winter's rest and winter encampment must not weaken idle hands through sluggishness; camp must be pitched on a hygienic site; a watchful guard must be posted on the ramparts' (*non brumae requies, non hibernacula segnes / eneruent torpore manus, ponenda salubri castra loco; praebenda uigil custodia uallo*).

[150] This lethargy is close to *the pleasure of* self-forgetting, cf. *iucunda* obliuia uitae, 'pleasant forgetfulness of life', Hor. *Serm.* 2. 6. 62 (with Stat. *Theb.* 1. 341; for *pigra Obliuio*, 'lazy Forgetfuln--', cf. ibid. 10. 89: on the threshold of the 'Palace of Sleep'). Vessey (1986) 2788 n. 118 recollects that '*obliuio uitae* suggests the blotting-out of memory that occurs on crossing Lethe' (Virg. *Aen.* 6. 715, 'They drink the liquid that takes away cares and swallow long forgetfulness', *securos latices et longa* obliuia *potant*); cf. Pitcher (1990), esp. 93 and n. 36, on the double-edged connotations of 'respite' *et sim.* in the *Siluae* (and in 1. 4).

[151] The verbal parallels are minor: fessos . . . *oculos*, inopi*na* quies laxauerat artus /, (Virg. *Aen.* 5. 845, 857); yet the lieutenant thought to have let himself get suckered from his post, but getting the chance to pop up from the dead, be praised and buried second time around, is a sure *conceptual* precedent for Statius' mythic Gallicus. Surreally enough, Gallicus is suffering from the chronic morbidity of Catullan obsession: 'like a narcosis creeping into the depths of the limbs' (76. 21, subrepens *imos ut torpor* in artus /: a hint of the serpent? Cf. Tib. 1. 1. 71, subrepet *iners aetas*, Vessey (1986) 2788 n. 118).

[152] Statius amplifies Gallicus' collapse to the dimension of national crisis, not least by echo of Horace's Pindaric Paean for Augustus to save Rome, *Carm.* 1. 2. 30–7, *tandem uenias precamur*, . . . *Apollo*, / siue tu . . . / siue neglectum *genus et nepotes* / respicis *auctor*, // heu . . .

[153] See esp. Malamud (1995), Masters (1996).

[154] Courtney (1990) xxi: 'This work, transmitted by a solitary fifteenth century manuscript, and that written by the most ignorant person of all that lived, has reached us everywhere deeply corrupted' (quoting Poggio's description of the copyist he used). Courtney lists twenty-five choice editions, and eighty-two *commentationes*.

[155] See esp. Reeve (1983) on the parlous transmission of the *Siluae*.

[156] Cf. Petrey (1990) 89ff. on the 'constative identity' of The King, whose power is brought into being by being hailed as Lord.

[157] It is often supposed that Horace's text was re-used by Domitian (e.g. D'Ambra (1993) 41), but 'A newly-made hymn is sung' (Zosimus 2. 5. 3, cf. the (conjectural) 'they sang a newly-composed song' for Septimius Severus (c[*arm*]en c[*ecinerunt noue c*]ompo[*situm*]), Pighi (1965) 227). We would surely know if Statius landed the commission previously won by Livius Andronicus, by P. Licinius Tegula, by Q. Horatius Flaccus (the only saecular poets we know).

[158] *Pace* Cairns (1972) 154: we shall return to this in chapter 19.

[159] Syme (1958) 97.

[160] Callim. *Hymn* 2. 39–41, 'Apollo's locks don't drip grease, / but Panacea herself. In any city where those / drops fall on the ground, everything turns healthy'.

[161] If we went in for analysis of myth as 'archetypal', Eliade (1963) would archetypally summarize for us: 24–8, 'The role of myths in healing': esp. 26, 'The close connection between the cosmogonic myth, the myth of the origin of a sickness and its remedy, and the ritual of magical healing . . .'; 39–53, 'Myths and Rites of Renewal': 42, 'There is always a cycle . . . Now, the end of one cycle and the beginning of the next are marked by a series of rituals whose purpose is the renewal of the World. . . . This *renovatio* is a re-creation after the model of the cosmogony'; 75–91, 'Time Can be Overcome': 85–8, 'Curing oneself of the work of Time', '*regressus ad uterum* is no longer practiced [*sic*] to obtain a cure or a rejuvenescence or even symbolic repetition of the cosmogony intended to heal the patient by reimmersing him in the primordial fullness . . . The[ ] final goal is not health or rejuvenation but spiritual mastery and liberation . . . Soteriologies . . . pursue ends other than magical cures'.

Must myth and its analysis always save the(ir) world for faith? From people like me?

[162] 'Callimachean' poetry regularly latches miniscule lyric on personal concerns to grand traditions and cosmic scope through linked temporalities, cf. Henderson (1995) on the tiny Horatian ode 3. 22.

[163] See Callim. *Hymn* 2, esp. 30f., 'Nor will the *choros* sing Phoebus for only one day /—for he is easy to hymn: who c/wouldn't sing Phoebus easily?', where *euumnos*, v. 31, cites *Hom. Hymn. to Apollo* 19, to take over for *his* synthesis *that* synthesis of (all) poetry under Apollo's poetic heaven, viz. all poetry.

[164] Intertextuality with Virgil's Land of the Dead comments on Apollo's unruly rhetoric. Wise Sibyl pre-empted his terms (*Aen.* 6. 125–31): 'Seed of the

blood of the gods, Trojan son of Anchises, easy is the way down to Hell: black Hades' door is ever wide. But to retrace your steps (*reuocare gradum*) and emerge to feel the breeze of the world above, that is the project, this is your task. A handful, those whom Jupiter the fair one has loved (*quos aequus amauit* / Iuppiter) or else their fiery courage has carrried them off and up to heaven's height, they have managed it, the sons of the gods (*dis geniti*)'. When Jupiter threatens to fuse with the god of the Underworld, this is a complaint against an outrageous cosmos, *not* a referential shift from Lord of Light to repulsive Dean of Death (as e.g. Vollmer (1971) 293 suggests for vv. 94f.).

165 Gallicus' own civil disobedience was (remember) down to his 'character' (vv. 44f.; 38, *morum*).

166 *Fila*: vv. 7, 64, 123.

167 Cf. Gallicus, v. 38: the way into hearts, deep and high as you can go!

168 A good idea, for a start, not to be a pleb., but to wear patrician purple. Otherwise, Statius wouldn't write you a *soteria* . . .

169 The would-be replacement for Nero, aristocratic Piso, is anti-type for (a) Gallicus, cf. *Laus Pison.* 2–6, 10f., 'Next your high birth and courage whirl me away, and your life miraculous in every way: this, if high birth had somehow happened to elude your beginnings, would have served for this high birth; all the prestige of a clan is lost in a man whose glory is in his origins alone'.

170 Cf. Woolf (1996) esp. 35. As we noticed (chapter 1), Gallicus' presumed equestrian origins and senatorial military tribunate (on the inscription) has figured persistently in attempts to sort out or leave entangled equestrian and senatorial career structures, cf. Demougin (1982) 91, 97: no. 13).

171 Domitian's grandfather Sabinus had been a 'distinguished' tax-collector in Asia; *his* father had run away from Pharsalus, to become a debt-collector: an 'obscure clan and with no higher magistrates among their ancestors', Suet. *Vesp.* 1. 1f.; 'he was neither of noble birth nor rich', Dio 65. 10. 3b (Zonaras). Sil. 3. 594–629 carves out a pre-destined Flavian future, cf. Henderson (1997) 139 n. 37: Vespasian, at least, 'laughed at fictions prettifying the origin of the Flavian clan', Suet. *Vesp.* 12. 2.

172 For the statesman's twin roles, cf. *Paneg. Mess.* 81f., 'your eloquence . . ., no other holds the skills of war more fitly than you', *Laus. Pison.* 39–66, 163–9; Tac. *Agr.* 4 prepares another *sublime et erectum ingenium* for his *prima castrorum rudimenta* (5. 1), cf. Stat. *Silu.* 4. 4. esp. 64f., Sherwin-White (1966) 181–3 on Plin. *Epp.* 2. 14.

173 For barbarian 'big bones', cf. Anderson (1938) 55 on Tac. *Germ.* 4. 2. Statius' phrase is eloquence itself—on 'eloquence'. Gauls grew, or dyed, *red* hair (Plin. *Nat. Hist.* 28. 191, Tac. *Hist.* 4. 61.1=rutil*atum*).

174 'Etymological word-play', or as I should say, professional soldier's ethic and credo, fits 'trained in camp', v. 72, *exercita castris*, for the 'army', *exercitus* (cf. Woodman (1977) 151, on Vell. 2. 109. 1, with 'regiment because it improves with regimen', Varr. *Ling. Lat.* 5. 87, *exercitus, quod exercitando fit melior*).

175 The *sacramentum* was probably renewed each New Year, Watson (1969) 48f.

[176] 'Through nine harvests', v. 77, recalls Catull. 95. 1, where the completion of Cinna's (*unmilitary*) epic, *Zmyrna*, is acclaimed: 'after the 9th harvest'. Is Statius using Volusius' *Annals*, as abused by Catullus?

[177] Cf. *Paneg. Mess.* 108–17, 138–50 for such globe-trotting mileage (esp. 'treacherous Pannonian', vv. 109f.).

[178] See Woolf (1996) esp. 33.

[179] Thrill to the news that a 'Gaul' is put 'in charge of the Gates of Rome' (*custodia Romae*, v. 16, cf. 91f.) *uae uictis* . . .! Shudder at the crack bodyguard of German troops arrayed around their *Germanicus*, the 'master' of Rome! If capture normed the 'curses of the mantic Leaderene' into the safe 'supplication of a captive enemy Chief' and the 'pleas of a harmless woman in chains', *weren't* her 'prayers' answered, as a *Germanicus* handed Rome for safe-keeping to a *Gallicus* (v. 90)?

[180] Cf. Theocr. 11; for the pun, cf. *Silu.* 2. 2. 20, van Dam (1986) 2735. In 84 Domitian had Apollo's temple at Delphi restored, and renovated (RE 4. 2579: ILS 8905). Apollo had repulsed Brennus' Celts from Delphi with bolt, quake . . . and [Alpine] *snow-blizzard* (Cic. *De div.* 1. 81, Prop. 3. 13. 51–4).

[181] Esp. *Carm.* 3. 5. 4. Cf. Nisbet and Hubbard (1970) 391 on Hor. *Carm.* 1. 35. 9 ('Russian retreat', and the steppes).

[182] The Araxes was 'named from its flattening everything with smash-and-grab' (as if from **arassô*, cf. Isid. *Orig.* 13. 21. 16, *dictus quod rapacitate cuncta prosternit*, Maltby (1991) 46). For shades of Alexander in the Araxes of Aeneas' shield, cf. 'Araxes a-bridged by Alex.' (Serv. *Auct.* on *Aen.* 8. 728, *Araxes cui Alexander Magnus pontem fecit*, with Hardie (1985) 28f., esp. n. 121). For the Virgilian river's typological resentment, see Quint (1993) 30f. Claudian is left to write: *impacatus Araxes* / ('Araxes still to be pacified', *Paneg. IV cos. Hon.* 8. 387!).

[183] Cf. Calvus, *Epigr.* fr. 18, *quid credas* hunc sibi uelle? *uirum.*

[184] Cf. Catull. 35. 9, '. . . though Snow White calls him back from his journey a thousand times' (*milies puella / euntem* reuocet), Ov. *Am.* 2. 18. 11, and other examples of Apollo yanking straying poets back on course (Wimmel (1960) 135–41): Statius' Apollo makes fun with another Callimachean topos featuring himself. There is verbal 'point' in *reuocant* <> *fasti* , as from *fari*, 'speak'.

[185] Cf. Mix (1970).

[186] *rebellis* is first extant in the Virgilian *locus* and rare thereafter; Statius conflates with Rhenusque *bicornis* / (*Aen.* 8. 727, 'the twin-horned Rhine').

[187] Veleda's successor, the virgin Ganna, visited Domitian Germanicus with King Masyos and returned home with honours (Dio 67. 5. 3); Vitellius Germanicus had 'a German prophetess' as 'part of his Imperator Germanicus set-up' (Murison (1992) 164 on Suet. *Vit.* 14. 5). Syme in *CAH* X: 158 assures us that Gallicus starred against the Bructeri, 'secur[ing] the person of Veleda' (for whom see Tac. *Hist.* 4. 61. 3 etc.).

[188] Most likely performed in 90/1, cf. *Silu.* 4. 2. 66f., *Germanas acies . . ., Daca . . . proelia.*

[189] Cf. *Silu* 1. 5. 29f., *quam . . . / pando domus*, for the gala opening of the baths; so at Petron. 89. 1, 'I shall try to open up a (siege-)work in verse'

(*conabor opus uersibus* pandere), frame and framed interpenetrate in the same way, for the *Troiae Halosis* poem that introduces a 'mob let loose from the gates' is halted by a hail of rocks from offended bystanders, as if playing the desperate population of an *Urbs capta*, e.g. Virg. *Aen.* 2. 445–9 (so, too, Ov. *Met.* 15. 622, / *pandere*, opening Rome to Aesculapius). In *Silu.* 1. 1. 11, Statius urbanely puns Domitian's equestrian statue (commemorating triumph over Germany and Dacia) into another Virgilian Wooden Horse invasion (*Aen.* 2. 234, *diuidimus muros et moenia* pand*imus* urb*is*, cf. Lühr (1880) 37): a 'good' match for his Prefect's 'defence' of the gates of Rome, in the pair of 'official' poems in *Siluae* I! (cf. chapter 20).

190 For the cave, cf. Pind. *Pyth.* 4. 181, 'For from the cave I come'; and (Apollo), '"Holy cave, son of Philura"', ibid. 9. 30. Ovid's Chiron dies of innocence of weapons; he gathers herbs, but is beyond saving by (his own) medical science (*Fasti* 5. 397–506, with Newlands (1995) 115f.).

   This chapter's title plays on Derrida (1981) 'Plato's Pharmacy', e.g. 70, 'This pharmakon, this "medicine", this philter, which acts as both remedy and poison . . . This charm, this spellbinding virtue, this power of fascination, can be—alternately or simultaneously—beneficent or maleficent . . .'.

191 Cf. [Tib.] 3. 7. 1f., 9f., 'Come to this place and drive out plague; come to this place, Phoebus, come your holiness and fetch with you whatever juices and whatever spells relieve exhausted bodies' (. . . *tecumque feras quicumque sapores,* / *quicumque et cantus corpora fessa leuant*).

192 Cf. Pind. *Nem.* 3. 55, 'Chiron; soft-handed régime', Cornutus *Theol. Gr.* 33, '"Chiron" because of his working with his hands', Robbins (1975) 211 and n. 20.

193 Cf. Edelstein and Edelstein (1945) Test. 436 (= Galen *Subfig. Emp.* 10) for a patient given snake-poison to swallow. Jackson (1988) 142 assures us, after Plin. *Nat. Hist.* 29. 72, Paus. 2. 28. 1 and Toynbee (1973) 224, that ancient snakes, including the yellow *anguis Aesculapius*, were harmless pets and zoo-curiosities when they were not beneficent guardians of the home, but this is, could it possibly be?, to insult divine thaumaturgy, cf. Padel (1992) 145f., 'They took snakes' healing power for granted. But they also lived with the possibility that gods might turn the snake's power against them at any moment. The fact that snakes might be divine did not make them any less dangerous. Snakes represent a multivalent threat to humanity, which matches their ambiguous mythic links with divine punishment and death'; cf. Weinreich (1908) 93–109.

194 ~ vv. 107f., *ritu se* cingit *uterque* / Paeonio, 101f.; cf. *herba . . . manu . . . herbis*, 402 ~ 99, 103; *non arte*, 427 ~ *non arte*, v. 112). Cf. nouae *rediere in pristina* uires ('strength returned to brand new'), 424 ~ reuirescit ('grows strong again'), v. 8, uires*que* nouas ('new strength'), v. 22. The cadence *sub umbra* /, v. 101, will always start*le* thoughts of Virgil (*Ecl.* 1. 1).

   In the (Flavian?) wall painting from Pompeii (Figure 8), Iapyx (from *iaomai*, 'heal'?) is short of Paeonian uniform, but plies steady pliers to display his manual skill, cf. '*Iapige*' in *EV* 883f.

195 In Mart. 9. 162, he is plain 'Pergamon's god'; cf. Krug (1985) 163–72, 'Rom und Pergamon', Price (1984) 148f., 252f., Habicht (1969) 7f. Earlier, the

Figure 8. Aeneas treated by Iapyx, wall-painting from Casa di Sirico, Pompeii (Museo Nazionale di Napoli *inv.* 9009).

Attalids had set their statues in the Temple (re-modelled *c.* 140–50 after Hadrian's Pantheon), which was in its heyday for the century before conflagration around 260, cf. Price (1984) 148, 'Fig. 6: The Sanctuary of Asclepius, Pergamum'; cf. de Fine Licht (1966) 226, 303 n. 144. At Rome, the *Collegium Aesculapi et Hygiae* would continue to meet 'in the temple of the immortalized in the shrine of immortalized Titus' (*ILS* 7213: the *Lex Collegii,* cf. Scott (1975) 63).

[196] Cf. Kee (1983) 78–104, 'Asclepios the Healer'. For the spread of the cult, cf. Garland (1992) 116–24: Pausan. 2. 26. 8 gives an aetiology tracing from Epidaurus to Pergamum. For 'applying a soft hand healing the wound', cf. Pind. *Pyth.* 4. 271, Weinreich (1908) 1ff., '*Theou Cheir*'; for the full range of treatments, cf. Padel (1992) 59f. on 'Asklepios Rizotomos', Dodds (1951) 115). On the reading and zeugma, or aposiopesis, in vv. 102f., *iungam . . . manus atque . . . benign-um/-e . . .,* cf. Vollmer (1971) 293, with Vessey (1986) 2788 n. 119.

[197] And it was to *Thymbraee* that Aeneas prayed when still thinking to re-found some toy Troy apology for a renaissance (*Aen.* 3. 85). Did Statius know that it was in this Temple that Achilles slew Troilus and was slain there in his turn? (Cf. Coleman (1988) 203 on *Silu.* 4. 7. 22–3, *Thymbrae.*)

[198] Cf. Liv. *Per.* 4, Parke (1988) 194f.

[199] Cf. Edelstein and Edelstein (1945), Habicht (1969) for Asklepios cult *testimonia.*

[200] Cf. Weinreich (1908) 38, e.g. Herodas 4. 18 (To Asklepios), 'O Lord, stretch out your mild hands', Cornutus *Theol. Gr.* 33., '"Asklepios" from mildly healing and deferring the "sclerosis" that comes with death'; Stat. *Silu.* 3. 4. 25.

[201] *Fasti* 1 and *Met.* 2 <> *Fasti* 6 and *Met.* 15, cf. esp. Newlands (1995) 42 n. 39. Jupiter's bolt also zapped Aesculapius at Verg. *Aen.* 7. 733.

[202] Cf. Luc. *Jup. Conf.* 8, Serv. *ad Aen.* 6. 398; at *Aen.* 7. 769, Diana assists 'with *Paeonian herbs*'. The *Fasti* finale fulfils the prophecy by Chiron's daughter in *Met.* 2. 642f. (Myers (1994) 135); such is poetic play with temporality re-scheduled, and such are 'the pragmatics of autocratic rule' (Newlands (1995) 194–6).

[203] See Keith (1992) 72–9, esp. 78f. and n. 35; on *urbi / orbi* here, Keith (1992) 72–4.

[204] Cf. Vivante (1972) esp. 112f., 'The action of Time will naturally be mellower, that of fate more definite, that of a god more personal. But these agencies melt into one another. My point is that, in such a context, time draws to itself the prerogatives of power. This is characteristic of Pindar. . . . It is as if the pressure of things to come forced [the Olympians] to act in the way they do.'

[205] Cf. Thomas (1988) Vol. 2, 37; Williams (1978) 49.

[206] This cooperation quotes from Ovid's family-and-staff twosome, Baucis and Philemon: 'the same pair obey and order' (Ov. *Met.* 8. 636, *idem parentque iubentque*).

[207] Statius' healing gods come to save another Aeneas 'war-hero', cf. vv. 106f., || *positos . . . artus* / pugnantem*que animam* ||, as they had in *Aen.* 12: by contrast, Iris comes to finish poor Dido off, *luct*antem animam || *nexosque resolueret* artus / (*Aen.* 4. 695).

[208] For the analysis, cf. 'I can't abide my limbs, this frail tenancy of the body, that runs out on the mind' (*Theb.* 8. 738 (Expiring Tydeus) *odi* artus *fragilemque hunc corporis usum,* / *desertorem* animi).

[209] *uolentes* (v. 108) playfully alludes to the prayer-formula requesting divine 'good will' (cf. Fraenkel (1950) on Aesch. *Ag.* 664, *thelon*).

[210] Cf. Vessey (1986) 2788 n. 120.

[211] Scarborough (1969) 104—whose Gallicus 'recovers at home under the care of his family'! He diagnoses Statian 'hypochondria' as symptomatic of the coming epoch (comparing *Silu.* 3. 5. 37–42, 5. 5. 42f.).

[212] In *arte . . . Haemonia* || and *Machaonio* || *. . . suco* /, 'the art of blood' (**haima*) runs together with 'the sap of battle', **mache*); Statius quotes from Ov. *Met.* 13. 171f., where Ulysses claims the credit, *ego Telephon hasta,* / *. . . refeci* /, *Ars* 2. 491, *Machaonios . . . sucos* / (linked to Apollo epiphany, cf.

Sharrock (1994) 233); and plays with Virgil's precursor at *Il.* 4. 217–19, 'when Machaon saw the wound where the poison arrow went in, he wiped off blood and skilfully spread over mild medicines that Chiron once afforded his father (Asklepios) in kindness'. Ancient critics complained that Menelaus acts like a kid and a softie, when, only grazed, he is fussed over by big brother and spells out there is no need for him or anyone to be afraid; Homer's slo-mo recounting of the relay from Agamemnon for Talthybius to fetch Machaon to treat the wound also attracted criticism for spoiling the drama of the emergency: healed by Virgil's lightning response, 'And there Iapyx was, Apollo's special favourite' (*Aen.* 12. 391; cf. Schlunk (1974) 90f. on Schol. *Il.* 4. 184; ibid. 91f. on Schol. *Il.* 4. 195). That other scene, *Iliadic* Apollo's healing of Glaukos' wound, is 'without the benefit of drugs', so Virgil 'modernized' his magic dittany by utilizing Theophrastus' account of the *Odyssey*'s wonder-herb *molu* (*Il.* 16. 527–32, *Od.* 10. 302–5, with Harrison (1990)).

[213] So 'Father of bards', v. 117; cf., too, 1. 2. 220, 'Leto's son, father of bards'. Marastoni (1958) 4 notes that properly respectful proportions are restored after these familiarities by the following simile of the dinghy Statius and the liner Gallicus; but cf. 'Sisters', v. 123.

[214] The *soteria* turns on this emotional disturbance, cf. Tib. 1. 5. 3ff. (anxious over sick Delia, and now sick, too, over her recovery after his rustic vows), 'I'm driven like a top whizzed across a flat spot by the lash'; Szelest (1971–2) 441, comparing Prop. 2. 28b. 39ff., Ps.-Tib. 3. 7. 11ff.

[215] Cf. 'The stars are my witnesses', Prop. 2. 9. 41; 'He never allows my door-posts rest', Prop. 1. 16. 15; on amatory 'fowling', Murgatroyd (1984). On the 'special association' of *adsiduus* with soldiers, cf. Cairns (1979) 17 and n. 71; for *uigil*, v. 119, cf. Gallicus' *uigiles . . . curae*, v. 55.

[216] A scaled-down re-working of Hor. *Epode* 1. 1f., where Maecenas' yacht is dwarfed by battleships? The similar simile in *Ciris* 478ff. captures the miniaturism that catches up poem, theme, and poetic altogether (cf. Lyne (1971) 246ff.).

[217] For the pattern 'Imperative, vocative, / repeat imperative', cf. Wills (1996) 92. 'Sisters', responds with 'father of bards', v. 117; but the absence of an honorific equivalent to *Thymbraee* (and to *Clotho*, v. 1, and *grauis inclementia fati*, v. 50) marks a shift in tonality (cf. *Epidauria proles <> nate*, vv. 61, 95).

[218] Various schemes are on offer, but for *formal* admiration, e.g. Cairns (1972) 154, Newmyer (1979) 93f.; see esp. Hardie (1983) 195f.

[219] For the topos cf. Coleman (1988) on *Silu.* 4. 2. 12, *sterilis . . . annos.*

[220] This assertion of worth is left short of its verb (vv. 125f.). Van Dam (1984) 258f. on *Silu.* 2. 2. 108 discusses Nestor/Priam/Tithonus complex(iti)es. The Sibyl's uncountable heap of years like dust particles alludes to Ov. *Met.* 14. 136.

[221] E.g. Tib. 2. 5. 40, 46, 61, cf. Cairns (1979) 76f.

[222] Herodas 4. 15; cf. 'The offerings to this god (Aesculapius) were chickens (*gallinae*)', Festus *s. v. insula*. For the Latin pun *gallus* = 'cock' / 'Gaul', cf. Suet. *Vit.* 9. 1, 15.3.

[223] Statius makes the hollow of his valley low with the round-up of cattle: ua*cuet* Meua*nia* ualles / aut . . . noualia tauros / (vv. 128f., cf. the onomatopoeic

uacca, 'cow'). From Virgil and Virgilian commentary, it became a fact (e.g. for Claudian) that these white bulls were the appointed victim at Roman triumphs, and a familiar piece of lore that cattle who drank or swam this fair river of Fame *gleamed*, cf. *niueos . . . boues*, Prop. 2. 19. 26, *candentis . . . tauros /*, Sil. 4. 546, cf. Thomas (1988) Vol. 1, 183 *ad loc.*

224 *caespes* and *salinum*, cf. Nisbet and Hubbard (1970) 242 on *Carm.* 1. 19. 13 and (1978) 250f. on *Carm.* 2. 16. 14; *exiguo*, cf. the prayer at Tibull. 1. 1. 33, with Wimmel (1960) 270f., 299; *far*, cf. the concluding nurse's prayer in Pers. 2. 75, *farre litabo*, with Williams (1969) 119 on *Carm.* 3. 23. 20, *farre pio et saliente mica. /*. The last word of 1. 4 leaves us with a dash of lyric 'wit' (*sal*) to liven up the pieties.

Statius is sure that *Horace* 'pleased the gods', starting with his tutelary curator, Maecenas, one of whose odes ends with a widow's mite from *his* poet (2. 17. 30–2), while another begins with 'incense' and 'turf altar', offered by the poet in thanksgiving (3. 8. 2–4, *acerra . . . caespite*; cf. 3. 23. 20, *farre pio et saliente mica*, Virg. *Aen.* 5. 745, *farre pio et plena . . . acerra /*, Lühr (1880) 13).

225 Cf. Callim. *Aitia* Prologue, for the seminal image of 'slender Muse and fattened sacrifice'. For 'Written in Haste', cf. Vessey (1986) 2761–5, with refs in 2762 n. 28.

226 E.g. Crotty (1982) 62.

227 Sontag (1983) 75, comparing Victorians' TB. Cf. Shilts (1988) in my Preface for AIDS.

228 A (very) well-read Stella might hear himself flattered as a 'Brutus' to Statius' 'Cicero' in the echo here of (the end of) the first sentence of the *Orator*.

239 Our MS has space for 13 missing letters here.

230 vv. 8f.: 'But a pause in the infectious carnage of guilty Thebes' (*paulum arma nocentia, Thebae, / ponite*). Just time to shower *chez* Claudius Etruscus. At the dramatic 'date' of 3. 2. 142f., Statius has 'still' not quite sold the city his *amica Thebais* (as Juvenal nicely-nastily describes the epic's publication, 7. 82f.).

231 Cf. Henderson (1991).

232 When Statius begins the poetry of *Siluae* with address to *Germanice* (1. 1. 5), he also resumes the authority he assumed *c.* 85–6 for his dashing epic *De Bello Germanico* (*not* signalled by *Praefatio*).

233 Engagingly or not, *Preface* is so wrapped up in the book's feats of 'w. p. m.' speed-writing that it blatantly *parades* lack of concern either with Gallicus' recent decease or with ambitious poetic programming of the collection. Vessey (1986) 2786 is *not* amused: 'Poems on this topic are uncommon in any age. There is always the risk that, as in this instance, the amelioration will prove temporary. Inevitably, the spirit of rejoicing has a hollow ring, if we read the poem realistically.'

234 Cf. the notorious 'problem' of Hor. *Carm.* 4. 12, where Virgil plays the undead.

235 Cairns (1972) 154, exploring the rhetoric of 'Reaction' through 'the rhetorical prescription for *soteria*': 'The fact that the *soteria* is eucharistic and presupposes a cure implies that the illness and cure will normally be narrated in examples of the genre as past occurrences. . . . [T]he logic of the

soteria guarantees . . .'. Vessey (1986) 2786 tartly observes: 'An epicedion would by now have been more in order'.

236 Inspired by Derrida (1981), and Bergren (1981), Segal (1986) practises good 'pharmacological' reading (of Pindar), cf. esp. 30, 'the double possibility inherent in all artifice of language: its poison of duplicity and its healing drug of truth . . . This poetry reveals the potential instability or reversibility of the elements by which it exercises this power over us: hence the ambiguity of the drugs or craft that serve as the metaphorical or symbolic correlates of poetry.' Norris (1987) 37 explains clearly.

237 In 'Polycharmus, just the once', the name-pun accurately defines the *soteria* as 'Multiplication of joy at one go' (as Stephen Hinds points out). Beside the *titulus* to *Silu.* 1. 4, this is the only appearance of the word *soteria* in extant Latin (here in the sense of 'offerings in thanks for regaining good health').

238 On such 'Performing the Performative', cf. Petrey (1990) 110, 'As Fish pointed out, . . . a very great deal rides on the "agreement (forever being renewed) to say 'Good Morrow'"'). Vessey (1986) 2785 also proposes *salus* as the conceptual matrix for 1. 4.

239 So (too) Auson. *Griph. Praef.*

240 Federspiel (1984) 45.

241 Eck (1970) 108 accepts Stella (from 1. 2. 71) along with Vopiscus of 1. 3 as a Flavian elevation to the patriciate. This may be over-literal. On Statius' Stella, cf. Syme (1988) 384f. His homonymous grandfather may have been a Praetorian Prefect of Gaius, and (?) organizer of Nero's first Games (Wiseman (1991) 69).

242 As praetor in 93, Stella was shortly or about to put on Domitian's Hyperborean victory games over the Sygambri (Mart. 8. 78). We should compare Horace's *Carmina* IV, where the poet-priest glosses his saecular song to refloat temporality *passim*: e.g. dedicating his central eighth poem to (the aptly named) Censorinus, who is named only after Agrippa among the *XVuiri s. f.* for Augustus' *ludi saeculares* (unless he is the son of same: such slippage itself embodies the re-cycling of names which regenerated *Roman Life* through the *gens*), and following this with another of the *XVuiri*, Lollius, for the ninth poem's meditation on time and ephemerality (cf. Putnam (1986) 155; Censorinus and Lollius would in time die in succession, Vell. 2. 102. 1, Woodman (1977) 128).

243 For the intrication of Tib. 2. 5, acclaiming Messalinus' enrolment as *XVuir s. f.*, with Virg. *Ecl.* 4's Sibylline/consular annunciation of the new world born with the child of destiny, cf. Cairns (1979) esp. 84ff. Constellations twinkle all over *Siluae* I.

244 On Statius' Vopiscus (?P.? Manilius, *PIR*² 5. 158, M. 141), cf. Syme (1988) 98f. His *uilla* is a Horatian haven in Horace's favourite Tibur, which, no doubt, inspires Statius to greater poesie (1. 3) than his host, who does not heed Horace (and Pindar) but instead emulates him (them) (cf. Newlands (1988) 107, reading through 1. 3. 101 to Hor. *Carm.* 4. 2. 1ff.).

245 Cf. Stat. *De Bell. Germ.*, *ap.* Valla (from Probus) on Juv. 4. 94, *Nestorei mitis prudentia Crispi*; for Nestor/Priam similes in the panegyric of well-wishing, cf. *Paneg. Mess.* 49f., 112, Sauter (1934) 117f.

140

246 I do not myself accept that Statius inserted the various 'titles' between his *Siluae*, as *Soteria Rutili Gallici* for 1. 4 (cf. van Dam (1984) 70f., Coleman (1988) xxviiiff., Damon (1990) 271 n. 7).

247 Cf. 'Books need a prayer to close with; fix successors as far in the future as may be', Vell. 2. 131 (but the MSS abort the prayer before it can be made, ending suitably with, 'and the plans of all citizens, either pious ones [--', and suppressing 'help, impious ones smash' *vel sim.* (or indeed 'Vell. *sim.*'). An eloquent chance, 'in a prayer devoted to political stability', Woodman (1977) 282 *ad loc.*). 'Statius' even 'stands for stability' (cf. *Lib. de praen.* 4, *Statius a stabilitate* (Maltby (1991) 581)!

248 *Siluae* I–III are all hexametric except for the final poems of I and II in hendecasyllables.

249 On Hor. *Carm.* 1. 2 as Pindaric Paean blended into saecular sacrality, see Cairns (1971) 84ff. For intertextuality between *Siluae* I(-III) and *Carmina* I-III, cf. Lühr (1880) 13, 24.

250 Coleman (1988) xvif. marshals the telling arguments for Statius' having gathered *Siluae* I-III en bloc, after Horace's *Carmina* I-III (and Ovid's *Amores*).

251 Cf. Rudd (1976) 117.

252 Read this climb-down as *both* the modal signal of a lighter key *and* as the mark of a territorial incursion by poetic grandeur. So when Apollo brought his train *down* from Helicon to colonize the hills of Rome for Stella's wedding, he went for it, with 277 hexameters for (t)his wedding-song (over twice the bulk of the other poems). Contrast Apollo's laconic dash through Gallicus' *Life* in the panic of 1. 4.

253 Claudius Etruscus was son of an imperial freedman from Smyrna, heir to the poshest of fake names (*PIR*³ 2. 200, C. 860).

254 *Carm.* 1. 5–6, cf. Santirocco (1986) 34. Contrast Chiron's 'cave' with the bath-house's 'cave', v. 98, 1. 5. 30.

255 Cf. Hor. *Carm.* 1. 29. 7f., *puer . . . ad cyathum*. But the most fun in Statius' *iunge puer cyathos* is the uncanny blur of Hor. *Carm.* 3. 8. 13, *sume Maecenas* cyathos *amici / sospitis* with the notorious pique of Calp. Sic. 4. 23, *frange* puer *calam*os, where one poet aspirant cites his fellow in frustration that their 'Maecenas' figure has not made a Virgil or Horace of them—not yet. (Rudd (1976) 93 ladles a reservoir of Juvenal–Martial–Calpurnius-Virgil *Ecl.* intertextuality from the phrase.)

256 Bright (1980) 57f.

257 Cf. Adams (1995), esp. 146f.

258 Statius' *lyra* tries to twang its hardest for Gallicus, 4. 36; his *chelys* is light for Etruscus, 5. 1, 11; Apollo plucks for Stella's wedding, brings a *chelys* for wedding-present and the Muses play a *lyra* each, 1. 2. 1, 226, 250. The most developed panoply of poetry/culture in the book, glossing the book as show-piece of poetry-culture, is the central villa-scene: pondered meditation in Epicurus' style; the *chelys* echoing in the Tibur sung by the greats, Virgil and Horace; the *lyra maior*, to Pindaric plucking or to epic *chelys*; to nightshade satire or to sparkling epistolography, 3. 90–104. These strains chart the chords of *Siluae* I.

[259] This displayed Virgilian tag is from *Georg.* 4. 176, but cf. *Ecl.* 1. 23, too, Lühr (1880) 33.

[260] Cf. Sil. 3. 614–21 in chapter 8, Plin. *Nat. Hist., Praef.* 5, Stat. *Theb.* 12. 814, *Ach.* 1. 15f., Suet. *Dom.* 2. 2 with Jones (1996) 22 *ad loc.*, Coleman (1986).

[261] Neither Brozek (1965), Most (1990) 14, nor Szelest (1972) (who compares (at 316) 1. 4's Apollo with Venus' intervention in 1. 2. 51–140) contemplates any such connection. Verstraete (1983) 201f. is content to remark the 'realism' of the description of Gallicus' illness and self-help (vv. 54f., 112f.) to offset the 'mythological fantasy' of Apollo's intervention.

[262] Cf. Val. Max. 6. 8. 4; Kokkinos (1992) 67.

[263] Nisetich (1980) 167. On this contentious Ode, cf. esp. Young (1968) 27–68, esp. 39f., 'Pythian 3 is a poem entirely concerned with disease, the healing of disease, and death'; Lefkowitz (1976) 142–57, Pelliccia (1987), Crotty (1982) 49–51.

[264] Cf. Mullen (1982) 101, 'All five examples of punishment outside the epode occur in *P.* 3', cf. 104.

[265] Mullen (1982) 131.

[266] So Young (1968) 62, 'Poetic immortality works'.

Bibliography

Works Referred to in the Text and Notes

Note: Standard works of reference are abbreviated as follows: *BMCRE=Coins of the Roman Empire in the British Museum*, see Mattingly (1930); *CAH=The Cambridge Ancient History*. see Bibliography *s. v.*; *CIL=Corpus Inscriptionum Latinarum*. ed. T. Mommsen, etc. (1862–, Berlin); *EOS=Epigrafia e Ordine Senatorio*, see Bibliography *s. v.*; *EV=Enciclopedia Virgiliana* (1985, Rome); *FCIR=Fasti Consolari dell' Impero Romano*=Degrassi (1952); *IE=Die Inschriften von Ephesos*, see Engelmann, etc. (1980); *ILS*: see Dessau (1892–1916); *LIMC=Lexikon Iconographicum Mythologiae Classicae* I. 1 (1981), II. 1 (1984, Zurich); *PIR=Prosopographia Imperii Romani*[2/3], I–II ed. E. Groag and A. Stein (1933, 1936, Berlin), III ed. P. de Rohden and H. Dessau (1978, Berlin), V ed. L. Petersen (1970–87, Berlin); *PME=Prosopographia militiarum equestrium*, see Devijver (1976); *RE=Real-Encyclopädie der classischen Altertumswissenschaft* ('Pauly-Wissowa').

Adams, B. (1995) *Timewatch. The Social Analysis of Time*, Cambridge.
Alföldy, G. (1982) 'Senatoren aus Norditalien *Regiones* IX, X und XI', in *EOS* (1982) II. 309–68.
Anderson, J. G. C. (1938) *Cornelii Taciti* De origine et situ Germanorum, Oxford.
Beard, M. (1991) 'Writing and religion: ancient literacy and the function of the written word in Roman religion. Question: What was the role of writing in Graeco-Roman paganism?', in *Literacy in the Roman World, Journal of Roman Archaeology Supplementary Series* 3, Ann Arbor.
Bendinelli, G. (1929) *Torino Romana*, Turin.
Bergren, A. L. T. (1981) 'Helen's "Good drug", *Odyssey* iv, 1–305', in Kresic (1981) 201–14.
Birley, A. R. (1982) 'Notes on senators' imperial service', in *EOS* (1982) I. 239–49.

Boyle, A. J. ed. (1990) *The Imperial Muse Volume 2. Flavian Epicist to Claudian,=Ramus* 18 (1989), Berwick, Victoria.
—— ed. (1993) *Roman Epic*, London.
—— ed. (1995) *Roman Literature and Ideology,=Ramus* 23 (1994) Berwick, Victoria.
Braithwaite, A. W. (1927) *C. Suetoni Tranquilli* Divus Vespasianus, *with an Introduction and Commentary*, Oxford.
Bright, D. F. (1980) *Elaborate Disarray. The Nature of Statius' "Silvae"*, Beiträge zur klassischen Philologie 108, Meisenheim am Glan.
Brind' Amour, P. (1978) 'L'origine des Jeux Séculaires', *Aufstieg und Niedergang der Römischen Welt* II. 16. 2. 1334–417.
Brozek, M. (1965) 'De Statio Pindarico', *Eos* 55. 338–40.
Buttrey, T. V. (1975) 'Domitian's perpetual censorship and the numismatic evidence', *Classical Journal* 71. 26–34.
CAH (1934) X: *The Cambridge Ancient History X. The Augustan empire 44 BC–AD 70*, Cambridge.
—— (1936) XI: *The Cambridge Ancient History XI. The Imperial Peace AD 70–192*, Cambridge.
Cairns, F. (1971) 'Horace, *Odes* 1. 2', *Eranos* 69. 68–88.
—— (1972) *Generic composition in Greek and Roman poetry*, Edinburgh.
—— (1979) *Tibullus. A Hellenistic Poet at Rome*, Cambridge.
—— (1984) 'Propertius and the battle of Actium', in Woodman and West (1984) 129–68.
—— (1992) 'The power of implication: Horace's invitation to Maecenas (*Odes* I. 20)', in Woodman and Powell (1992) 84–109.
Carter, J. M. (1982) *Suetonius, Diuus Augustus, edited with Introduction and Commentary*, Bristol.
Cavaliere Manasse, G., G. Massari and M. P. Rossignani (1982) *Guide Archeologiche Laterza. Piemonte, Valle d'Aosta, Liguria, Lombardia*, Rome.
Chilver, G. E. F. (1941) *Cisalpine Gaul*, Oxford.
Christol, M. and S. Demougin (1985) 'Notes de prosopographie equestre. III. C. Rutilius Secundus, procurateur de Mauretanie Tingitane?', *Zeitschrift für Papyrologie und Epigraphik* 59. 283–90.
Coleman, K. M. (1986) 'The emperor Domitian and literature', *Aufstieg und Niedergang der Römischen Welt* II. 32. 5. 3087–115.
—— (1988) *Statius Silvae IV, edited with an English Translation and Commentary*, Oxford.
Courtney, E. ed. (1990) *P. Papinii Stati* Siluae, Oxford.
Cresci Marroni, G. and E. Culasso Gastaldi, eds (1988) *Per pagos uicosque. Torino Romana fra Orco e Stura, Saggi e Materiali Universitari 11, Serie di Antichità e Tradizione classica* 10, Padova.
Crook, J. (1955) Consilium principis. *Imperial Councils and Counsellors from Augustus to Diocletian*, Cambridge.
Crotty, K. (1982) *Song and Action. The Victory Odes of Pindar*, Baltimore.
Culasso Gastaldi, E. (1988) 'Romanizzazione subalpina tra Persistenze e Rinnovamento', in Cresci Marroni and Culasso Gastaldi (1988) 219–29.

Currie, H. Macl. (1996) 'Horace's "Epigraphic poetry": some comments on *Odes* IV', *Latomus* 55. 79–86.

van Dam, H.-J. (1984) *P. Papinius Statius* Silvae *Book II. A Commentary*, Mnemosyne Supplementum 82, Leiden.

—— (1986) 'Statius, *"Silvae"*. Forschungsbericht 1976–1984', *Aufstieg und Niedergang der Römischen Welt* II. 32. 5. 2727–53.

D'Ambra, E. (1993) *Private Lives, Imperial Virtues: The Frieze of the Forum Transitorium in Rome*, Princeton.

Damon, C. (1990) 'Poem division, paired poems, and *Amores* 2. 9 and 3. 11', *Transactions of the American Philological Association* 120. 269–90.

Davis, L. (1992) *The Iron Hand of Mars*, London.

Degrassi, A. (1952) *I Fasti Consolari dell' Impero Romano*, Rome.

Demougin, S. (1982) '*Uterque ordo*. Les rapports entre l'ordre senatorial et l'ordre equestre sous les Julio-Claudiens', in *EOS* (1982) I. 73–104.

Derrida, J. (1981) *Dissemination*, London.

Desjardins, E. (1877) 'Nécessité des connaissances epigraphiques pour l'intelligence de certains textes classiques. Lettre à M. Havet sur la IVe *Silve* du Ier livre de Stace', *Révue de Philologie* 1. 7–24.

—— (1877A) 'Note additionelle, sur la IVe *Silve* du Ier livre de Stace. Seconde lettre à Louis Havet', *Révue de Philologie (RPh)* 1. 189–92.

Dessau, H. (1892–1916) *Inscriptiones Latinae Selectae* [=*ILS*], *I–III.2*, Berlin.

Devijver, H. (1976) *Prosopographia militiarum equestrium quae fuerunt ab Augusto ad Gallienum* [=*PME*], Pt. 1, Louvain.

Dewar, M. (1991) *Statius' Thebaid IX*, Oxford.

Dodds, E. R. (1951) *The Greeks and the Irrational*, Berkeley.

Dudley, D. R. ed. (1972) *Neronians and Flavians. Silver Latin I*, London.

Dunston, A. J. (1967), 'What Politian saw: Statius, *Siluae* I. 4. 88', *Bulletin of the Institute of Classical Studies* 14. 96–101.

DuQuesnay, I. M. Le M. (1976) 'Vergil's Fourth *Eclogue*', *Proceedings of the Liverpool Latin Seminar* 1. 25–99.

—— (1984) 'Horace and Maecenas: the propaganda value of *Sermones* I', in Woodman and West (1984) 19–58.

Duret, L. (1986) 'Dans l'ombre des plus grands: II. Poètes et prosateurs mal connus de la Latinité d'Argent', *Aufstieg und Niedergang der Römischen Welt* II. 32. 5. 3152–346.

During, S. (1992) *Foucault and Literature. Towards a Genealogy of Writing*, London.

Eck, W. (1970) *Senatoren von Vespasian bis Hadrian: prosopographische Untersuchungen*, Vestigia 13, Munich.

—— (1972) 'Bemerkungen zum Militärkommando in den Senatsprovinzen der Kaiserzeits', *Chiron* 2. 429–36.

—— (1984) 'Senatorial self-representation: developments in the Augustan period', in Millar and Segal (1984) 129–67.

—— (1985) 'Statius *Silvae* 1.4 und C. Rutilius Gallicus als *proconsul Asiae* II', *American Journal of Philology* 106. 475–84.

Edelstein, E. J. and L. (1945) *Asclepius: A Collection and Interpretation of the Testimonies. Volumes 1–2*, Baltimore.

Eliade, M. (1963) *Myth and Reality*, New York.

Engelmann, H., D. Knibbe, R. Merkelbach, eds (1980) *IE [=Die Inschriften von Ephesos]* III=*Inschriften griechischer Städte aus Kleinasiens XIII*, Bonn.

EOS (1982)=*Atti del Colloquio Internazionale A. I. E. G. L. su Epigrafia e Ordine Senatorio. Roma 14–20 maggio 1981*, Rome.

Federspiel, J. F. (1984) *The Ballad of Typhoid Mary*, London.

de Fine Licht, K. (1966) *The Rotunda in Rome. A Study of Hadrian's Pantheon*, Jutland Archaeological Society Publications 8.

Fishwick, D. (1987) *The Imperial Cult in the Latin West. Studies in the Ruler Cult of the Western Provinces of the Roman Empire. Volume 1*, EPRO [Etudes préliminaires aux Religions orientales dans l'Empire Romain] 108, Leiden.

Foss, C. (1979) *Ephesus after Antiquity: A Late Antique, Byzantine and Turkish City*, Cambridge.

Foulon, A. (1983) 'Tibullus, II, 5: Hellénisme et Romanité', *Révue des Etudes Latines* 61. 173–88.

Fraenkel, E. (1950) *Aeschylus, Agamemnon, Edited with a Commentary*, Oxford.

Frezouls, E. (1994) 'Domitien et l'administration des provinces', *Pallas* 40. 301–28.

Friedländer, L. (1870) *De personis nonnullis a Statio commemoratis*, Regimonti.

—— (1880) *De C. Rutilio Gallico*, Regimonti.

—— (1881) *Darstellungen aus der Sittengeschichte Roms in der Zeit von August bis zum Ausgang der Antoninen, III. 5*, Leipzig.

Friesen, S. F. (1993) *Twice Neokoros. Ephesus, Asia and the Cult of the Flavian Imperial Family*, Leiden.

Frischauer, W. (1960) *The Rise and Fall of Hermann Goering*, London.

Fry, P. H. (1980) *The Poet's Calling in the English Ode*, Yale.

Garland, R. (1992) *Introducing New Gods*, London.

Gossage, A. J. (1972) 'Statius', in Dudley (1972) 184–235.

Griffin, M. T. (1976) *Seneca: a philosopher in politics*, Oxford.

—— = M. T. G. (1990) 'Sir Ronald Syme, 1903–1989', *Journal of Roman Studies* 80. xi–xiv.

Groag, E. (1920) 'Rutilius 19)' in *RE* 1A. 1255–63.

Gsell, S. (1967) *Essai sur le règne de l'Empereur Domitien*, Studia Historica 46, Rome.

Habicht, C. (1969) *Die Inschriften des Asklepieions, D. A. I. Altertumer von Pergamon* VIII. 3. x, Berlin.

Hardie, A. (1983) *Statius and the Silvae. Poets, Patrons and Epideixis in the Graeco-Roman World*, Liverpool.

Hardie, P. R. (1985) '*Imago mundi*: cosmological and ideological aspects of the shield of Achilles', *Journal of Hellenic Studies* 105. 11–31.

Harrison, S. J. (1990) '*Dictamnum* and *moly*: Vergil *Aeneid* 12. 411–19', *Proceedings of the Leeds Latin Seminar* 6. 45–7.

Henderson, B. W. (1927) *Five Roman emperors. Vespasian. Titus. Domitian. Nerva. Trajan, AD 69–117*, Cambridge.

Henderson, J. (1990) 'Tacitus/The World in Pieces', in Boyle (1990) 167–210.

—— (1991) 'Statius' *Thebaid*/ Form premade', *Proceedings of the Cambridge Philological Society* 37. 30–80.

—— (1994) 'On getting rid of kings: Horace *Satires* 1. 7', *Classical Quarterly* 44. 146–70.

—— (1995) 'Horace, *Odes* 3.22 and the life of meaning: stumbling and stampeding out of the woods, / blinking and screaming into the light, / snorting and gorging at the trough, / slashing and gouging at the death', *Ramus* 24. 103–51.

—— (1997) *Figuring out Roman nobility. Juvenal's Eighth* Satire, Exeter.

Hopkins, K. (1991) 'Conquest by book', in *Literacy in the Roman world*, *Journal of Roman Archaeology Supplement* 3, Ann Arbor, 133–58.

Hosek, C. and P. Parker, eds (1985) *Lyric Poetry. Beyond New Criticism*, Ithaca.

Hubbard, T. K. (1984) ' Art and vision in Propertius 2.31/2', *Transactions of the American Philological Association* 114. 281–97.

Jackson, R. (1988) *Doctors and Diseases in the Roman Empire*, London.

Jacobus, M. (1985) 'Apostrophe and lyric voice in *The Prelude*', in Hosek and Parker (1985) 167–81.

Jones, B. W. (1979) *Domitian and the senatorial order. A prosopographical Study of Domitian's Relationship with the Senate, AD 81–96*, Memoirs of the American Philosophical Association 132, Philadelphia.

—— (1992) *The Emperor Domitian*, London.

—— (1996) *Suetonius* Domitian, *Edited with Introduction and Notes*, Bristol.

Kähler, H. (1942) 'Die römische Torburgen der frühen Kaiserzeit', *Jahrbuch des Deutschen Instituts* 57. 1–104.

Kee, H. C. (1983) *Miracles in the Early Christian World. A Study in Sociohistorical Method*, Yale.

Keil, J. (1914) 'Eine neue Inschrift des C. Rutilius Gallicus aus Ephesos', *Jahresheftes des österreichischen Archäologischen Instituts in Wien* 17. 194–9.

Keith, A. M. (1992) *The Play of Fictions. Studies in Ovid*, Metamorphoses *Book II*, Ann Arbor.

Keppie, L. (1983) *Colonisation and Veteran Settlement in Italy 47–14 BC*, London.

Kilpatrick, R. S. (1986) *The Poetry of Friendship. Horace,* Epistles *I*, Alberta.

Knox, B. M. W. (1950) 'The serpent and the flame. The imagery of the Second Book of the *Aeneid*', *American Journal of Philology* 71. 379–400.

Kokkinos, N. (1992) *Antonia Augusta. Portrait of a Great Roman Lady*, London.

Kresic, S. ed. (1981) *Contemporary literary hermeneutics and the Interpretation of Classical Texts*, Ottawa.

Krug, A. (1985) *Heilkunst und Heilkult. Medizin in der Antike*, Munich.

Lefkowitz, M. R. (1976) *The Victory Ode. An Introduction*, New Jersey.

Lewis, M. W. H. (1955) *The Official Priests of Rome under the Julio-Claudians. A Study of the Nobility from 44 BC to 68 AD*, Papers and Monographs of the American Academy in Rome 16.

Lühr, G. (1880) *De P. Papinio Statio in* Siluis *priorum poetarum Romanorum imitatore*, Königsberg.

Lyne, R. O. A. M. (1971) 'The dating of the *Ciris*', *Classical Quarterly* 21. 233–53.

McDermott, W. C (1949) '*Sextus Afranius Burrus*', *Latomus* 8. 229–45.

McDermott, W. C. and A. E. Orentzel (1979) *Roman Portraits. The Flavian-Trajanic Period*, Columbia.

MacDonald, W. (1982) *Architecture of the Roman Empire, I*, Yale.

MacMullen, R. (1982) 'The epigraphic habit in the Roman empire', *American Journal of Philology* 103. 233–46.

—— (1984) 'The legion as society', *Historia* 33. 440–56.

Malamud, M. A. (1995) 'Happy birthday, dead Lucan: (P)raising the dead in *Silvae* 2. 7', in Boyle (1995) 169–98.

Maltby, R. (1991) *A Lexicon of Ancient Latin Etymologies*, Liverpool.

Marastoni, A. (1958) 'Per una nuova interpretazione di Stazio Poeta delle Selve. II', *Aevum* 32. 1–37.

Martin, R. H. and A. J. Woodman (1989) *Tacitus* Annals *Book IV, edited*, Cambridge.

Martinelli, L. C. (1978) *A. Poliziano. Commento inedito alle Selve di Stazio*, Florence.

Masters, H.V. (1996) 'After the Battle. A Comparison of Lucan and Statius with Regard to Battlefields, Bodies and Burial', unpublished Cambridge MPhil thesis.

Mattingly, H. (1930) *Coins of the Roman Empire in the British Museum* [=*BMCRE*] 2. *Vespasian to Domitian*, London.

Mayor, J. E. B. (1886⁴) *Thirteen Satires of Juvenal*, London.

Merkelbach, R. (1979) 'Ephesische Parerga 26: Warum Domitians Siegername "Germanicus" eradiert worden ist', *Zeitschrift für Papyrologie und Epigraphik* 34. 62–4.

Meyer, E. A. (1990) 'Explaining the epigraphic habit in the Roman empire: the evidence of epitaphs', *Journal of Roman Studies* 80. 74–96.

Millar, F. (1977) *The Emperor in the Roman World*, London.

Millar, F. and E. Segal, eds (1984) *Caesar Augustus. Seven aspects*, Oxford.

Mittelstadt, M. C. (1968) 'The plague in Thucydides: an extended metaphor?', *Rivistà di Studi Classici, Torino* 16. 14–54.

Mix, E. R. (1970) *M. Atilius Regulus: exemplum historicum*, The Hague.

Most, G. W. (1990) *The Measures of Praise. Structure and Function in Pindar's Second* Pythian *and Seventh* Nemean *Odes*, Hypomnemata 83, Göttingen.

Mullen, W. (1982) *C H O R E I A: Pindar and Dance*, Princeton.

Murgatroyd, P. (1984) 'Amatory hunting, fishing and fowling', *Latomus* 43. 362–8.

Murison, C. L. (1992) *Suetonius Galba, Otho, Vitellius, Edited with introduction and notes*, Bristol.

Myers, K. S. (1994) *Ovid's Causes. Cosmogony and Aetiology in the* Metamorphoses, Ann Arbor.

Newlands, C. E. (1988) 'Horace and Statius at Tibur: an interpretation of *Silvae* 1. 3', *Illinois Classical Studies* 13. 95–111.

—— (1995) *Playing with time. Ovid and the* Fasti, Ithaca.

Newmyer, S. T. (1979) *The* Silvae *of Statius. Structure and Theme*, Mnemosyne Supplementum 53, Leiden.

Nisbet, R. G. M. and M. Hubbard (1970) *A Commentary on Horace:* Odes *Book I*, Oxford.
—— (1978) *A Commentary on Horace:* Odes *Book II*, Oxford.
Nisetich, F. (1980) *Pindar's Victory Songs*, Baltimore.
Norris, C. (1987) *Derrida*, London.
Padel, R. (1992) *In and Out of the Mind. Greek Images of the Tragic Self*, Princeton.
Parke, H. W. (1988) *Sibyls and Sibylline Prophecy in Classical Antiquity*, London.
Pascal, C. B. (1964) *The Cults of Cisalpine Gaul*, Collection Latomus 75.
Pelliccia, H. (1987) '*Pindarus Homericus*: Pythian 3.1–80', *Harvard Studies in Classical Philology* 91. 39–63.
Petrey, S. (1990) *Speech Acts and Literary Theory*, London.
Pighi, J. B. (1965) *De ludis saecularibus populi Romani Quiritium libri sex*, Amsterdam.
Pitcher, R. A. (1990) 'The emperor and his virtues: the qualities of Domitian', *Antichthon* 24. 86–95.
Poe, J. P. (1984) 'The secular games, the Aventine, and the *pomerium* in the Campus Martius', *Classical Antiquity* 3. 57–81.
Price, S. R. F. (1984) *Rituals and Power. The Roman Imperial Cult in Asia Minor*, Cambridge.
Promis, C. (1869) *Storia dell' antica Torino*, Turin.
Putnam, M. C. J. (1986) *Artifices of Eternity. Horace's Fourth Book of Odes*, Ithaca.
Quint, D. (1993) *Epic and Empire. Politics and Generic Form from Virgil to Milton*, Princeton.
Reeve, M. D. (1983) 'Statius. *Siluae*', in Reynolds (1983) 397–9.
Reinhold, M. (1988) *From Republic to Principate. An Historical Commentary on Cassius Dio's* Roman History *Books 49–52 (36–29 BC)*, American Philological Association Monograph 34, Atlanta.
Reynolds, L. D. ed. (1983) *Texts and Transmission. A Survey of the Latin Classics*, Oxford.
Richardson, J. S. (1991) '*Imperium Romanum*: empire and the language of power', *Journal of Roman Studies* 81. 1–9.
Richardson Jr., L. (1992) *A New Topographical Dictionary of Ancient Rome*, Baltimore.
Richmond, I. A. (1943) 'Augustan gates at Torino and Spello', *Proceedings of the British School at Rome* 12. 52–62.
Ritterling, E. (1925) '*Legio*', *R.-E.* XII. 1. (1925) 1686–829.
—— (1927) 'Military forces in the senatorial provinces', *Journal of Roman Studies* 17. 28–32.
Robbins, E. (1975) 'Jason and Cheiron: the myth of Pindar's Fourth *Pythian*', *Phoenix* 29. 205–13.
Robinson, O. F. (1992) *Ancient Rome. City Planning and Administration*, London.
Rogers, G. M. (1991) *The Sacred Identity of Ephesos. Foundation Myths of a Roman City*, London.
Rudd, N. (1976) *Lines of Enquiry. Studies in Latin Poetry*, Cambridge.

Salomies, O. (1992) *Adoptive and Polyonomous Nomenclature in the Roman Empire*, Commentationes humanarum litterarum 97, Helsinki.

Santirocco, M. S. (1986) *Unity and Design in Horace's Odes*, Chapel Hill.

Sauter, F. (1934) *Der römische Kaiserkult bei Martial und Statius*, Tübinger Beiträge zur Altertumswissenschaft 21, Stuttgart.

Scarborough, J. (1969) *Roman Medicine*, London.

Schlunk, R. R. (1974) *The Homeric Scholia and the Aeneid. A Study of the Influence of Ancient Homeric Literary Criticism on Vergil*, Ann Arbor.

Scott, K. J. (1933) 'Statius' adulation of Domitian', *American Journal of Philology* 54. 247–59.

—— (1975=1936) *The Imperial Cult under the Flavians*, New York.

Segal, C. (1986) *Pindar's Mythmaking. The Fourth* Pythian *Ode*, Princeton.

Sharrock, A. R. (1994) *Seduction and Repetition in Ovid's* Ars Amatoria *II*, Oxford.

Sherwin-White, A. N. (1966) *The* Letters *of Pliny. A Historical and Social Commentary*, Oxford.

Shilts, R. (1988) *And the Band Played On. Politics, People, and the AIDS Epidemic*, Harmondsworth.

Sobel, H. (1990) *Hygieia. Die Göttin der Gesundheit*, Darmstadt.

Sontag, S. (1983) *Illness as Metaphor*, Harmondsworth.

Southern, P. (1997) *Domitian. Tragic Tyrant*, London.

Stern, J. (1970) 'The myth of Pindar's *Olympian 6*', *American Journal of Philology* 91. 332–40.

Syme, R. (1958) *Tacitus*, Oxford.

—— (1979–84) *Roman Papers I–III*, Oxford.

—— (1988) *Roman Papers IV–V*, Oxford.

—— (1991) *Roman Papers VI–VII*, Oxford.

Szelest, H. (1968) 'De P. Papinii Statii *Silvae* 1, 4 compositione et fontibus', *Meander* 23. 298–305.

—— (1971–2) 'Soteria Rutilii Gallici (Stat. *Silv.* I, 4)', *Helikon* 11–12. 433–43.

—— (1972) 'Mythologie und ihre Rolle in den "*Silvae*" des Statius', *Eos* 60. 309–17.

Thomas, R. F. (1988) *Virgil, Georgics I-IV. Volumes 1-2 Edited*, Cambridge.

Thomasson, B. E. (1982) 'Sullo Stato dei *legati censitores*', in *EOS* (1982) I. 305–18.

Toynbee, J. M. C. (1973) *Animals in Roman Life and Art*, London.

Verstraete, B. C. (1983) 'Originality and mannerism in Statius' use of myth in the *Silvae*', *L'Antiquité Classique* 52. 195–205.

Vessey, D. W. T. (1986) 'Transience preserved: style and theme in Statius' "*Silvae*"', *Aufstieg und Niedergang der Römischen Welt* II. 32.5. 2754–802.

Vidman, L. (1982) 'Osservazioni sui *Praefecti Urbi* nei primi due Secoli', in *EOS* (1982) I. 289–303.

Vigneaux, P. E. (1896) *Essai sur l'histoire de la* praefectura Urbis *à Rome*, Paris.

Vitucci, G. (1956) *Ricerche sulla* praefectura Urbi *in Età Imperiale (sec. I–III)*, Rome.

Vivante, P. (1972) 'On time in Pindar', *Arethusa* 5. 107–31.

Vollmer, Fr. F. (1971=1898) *Statius: Siluarum libri*, Hildesheim.

Watson, G. R. (1969) *The Roman Soldier*, London.
Weinreich, O. K. (1908) *Antike Heilungswunder*, *RGVV* 8.1, Giessen.
White, P. (1993) *Promised Verse. Poets in the Society of Augustan Rome*, Cambridge, Ma.
Williams, F. (1978) *Callimachus, Hymn to Apollo, a Commentary*, Oxford.
Williams, G. (1969) *The Third Book of Horace's Odes*, Oxford.
Wills, J. (1996) *Repetition in Latin Poetry. Figures of Allusion*, Oxford.
Wilson, M. (1993) 'Flavian variant: history. Silius' *Punica*', in Boyle (1993) 218–36.
Wimmel, W. (1960) *Kallimachos im Rom. Die Nachfolge seines apologetischen Dichtens in der Augusteerzeit*, Hermes Einzelschrift 16.
Wiseman, T. P. (1991) *Flavius Josephus. Death of an Emperor*, Exeter.
Woodman, A. J. (1977) *Velleius Paterculus. The Tiberian Narrative (2.94–131)*, Cambridge.
—— (1983) *Velleius Paterculus. The Caesarian and Augustan Narrative (2.41–93)*, Cambridge.
Woodman, T. and D. West eds. (1984) *Poetry and Politics in the Age of Augustus*, Cambridge.
Woodman, T. and J. Powell, eds (1992) *Author and Audience in Latin Literature*, Cambridge.
Woolf, G. (1996) 'Monumental writing and the expansion of Roman society in the early Empire', *Journal of Roman Studies* 8. 22–39.
Yardley, J. (1977) 'The Roman elegists, sick girls, and the *soteria*', *Classical Quarterly* 27. 394–401.
Young, D. C. (1968) *Three Odes of Pindar. A Literary Study of* Pythian 11, Pythian 3, *and* Olympian 7, Mnemosyne Supplementum 90, Leiden.
Zanker, P. (1988) *The Power of Images in the Age of Augustus*, Ann Arbor.

Indices

1. Chief Passages Discussed in the Text and Notes

2. General

[1] GRAECO–ROMAN MYTH:

[2] GREEK & LATIN WORDS:

Iapyx: n. 194; *iuuenile* = *to neanikon*: 63; *Machaon*: n. 212; *manet / manebit*: 47f., n. 112; *mitis*: 48, 55, 74, 92, n. 115; *Nomios*, 93; *opus*: 40, n. 98; *pando*: n. 189; *Piplea*: 54; *Pirene*: 54; *Polycharmus*: 107, n. 237; *praeceps*: 63; *Rutilius*: 83; *salus*: 48, 107; *senecta* = slough: n. 105; *sine numine (diuum)*: n. 129; *spumatus*: 90; *Statius*: n. 247; *Thymbra*: 92; *Virbius*: 92; *uoluo*: 84, n. 98.

[3] IMPERIAL GOVERNMENT:

Burden, of office: 43, n. 104; 'deuteragony' (deputizing for emperor): 25–32, 87, 110–12; Legions: V *Alauda*: 33; VII *Gemina*: 35; XIII *Gemina*: 7f., 11; XIV *Gemina*: n. 43; XV *Apollinaris*: 8, 11, 14, 18; Praetorian Prefect: 29; Urban Prefect: 25, 29f., 45, 48, 60, n. 4, n. 56, n. 107, n. 111, n. 144, wore *toga*: 60.

[4] PLACES:

See Figure 5 for maps. Africa: 18; Alps: 19f., 86; Amphrysos: 94; Araxes, R.: 84, n. 182; Ephesus: 11–15, n. 33, n. 36; Galatia: 17; Galatians: 22, 83f.; raid on Delphi: 83f.; Pergamum: 22, 91f., n. 195; Pamphylia: 84, n. 18; Seven Hills of Rome: 45, n. 109; Tarentum (Terentum?), Altar of: 49f., n. 110, n. 122; Thymbra: 92, n. 197; Turin: 19–24, n. 25, n. 42, n. 48, *Porta Palatina*: 22, n. 50, Figure 4.

[5] RELIGION:

'nosopolitics': 2, n. 5; poet–priest: 38, 74; polytheism: 39–42, 87, 93f.; prayer: as binding spell: 47f., 88–90, 97f., 106f., challenge to malevolent: 43, 45f., 50, 57, of/for community: 38–40, 42f., 45f., 48, 50, 73f., 87f., 97f., 106f., conditionality: 77–9, 100, 117f., *epiklesis*: 52–6, closural *gnome*: 98, 117, always precarious / conative / optative: 43, 45f., 53, 74, 98, 100f., 104–6, 117f., the 'widow's mite' (turf, spelt, salt-cellar: n. 224): 101; religion and writing: n. 93; saecular games: see Domitian; *soteria*: 39, 61, 74, 106f., n. 4, n. 214, n. 233, n. 235; transcendence: 76–9, 93f.

[6] RHETORIC:

anacolouthon: 63; composition, verse / prose: 54; litotes: 40, 84f., 87; parathesis: 43, 57, 63, 84; pharmacological reading: Preface, 105, n. 190, n. 236; prayer: see Religion.

[7] ROMANS:

Agrippa: 25, 27, 49, 113, n. 57; M. Arrecinus Clemens: 32, 33; T. Aurelius Fuluus: 27, 32; Brutus the Liberator: 60; Brutus the Tyrannicide: 60; Burrus (Sex. Afranius): 29, n. 66; Caecina Paetus (C. Laecanius Bassus): 10; Claudius Etruscus: 112f.; Corbulo (Cn. Domitius): 8, 32; Domitian: Chief Priest: 87, emperor worship: 38f., 42, 48f., 93, n. 4, n. 116, Father of the City: 87, and Minerva: 53, *Germanicus*: 18, 35, 42, n. 85, n. 232, rebuilt